THE POLITICAL BRAIN

CEU PRESS
PERSPECTIVES

How did we get to the precarious state that we find ourselves in today? What new thinking is needed to tackle the big problems we face? Offering the latest perspectives on both new and perennial issues, books in this series address a wide range of topics of critical importance. An international collection of leading authors encourages us to look at topics from different viewpoints; to think outside the box. Launched to commemorate 30 years of the CEU Press, the series looks to stimulate debates on the broader issues of the day.

Published in the series:

» Eric Fassin, *State Anti-Intellectualism and the Politics of Gender and Race: Illiberal France and Beyond*

» Per Högselius and Achim Klüppelberg, *The Soviet Nuclear Archipelago: A Historical Geography of Atomic-Powered Communism*

Forthcoming in the series:

» Raluca Bejan and Kristina Nikolova, *The Cold War Divide: COVID-19 Infection and Mortality Rates*

» András Bozóki, *The Role of Intellectuals in Society*

» Jeffrey C. Goldfarb, *Gray is Beautiful: Ten Lectures from the Radical Center on the Political Consequences of the Social Condition*

» Jie-Hyun Lim, *Victimhood Nationalism in Global Easts*

» Ranabir Samaddar, *Biopolitics from Below: Crisis, Conjuncture, Rupture*

The POLITICAL Brain

The Emergence of Neuropolitics

Matt Qvortrup

CEU PRESS

©2024 Matt Qvortrup

Published in 2024 by
Central European University Press

Nádor utca 9, H-1051 Budapest, Hungary
Tel: +36-1-327-3138 or 327-3000
E-mail: ceupress@press.ceu.edu
Website: www.ceupress.com

Printed and bound by CPI Group (UK) Ltd, Croydon, CR0 4YY

ISBN 978-963-386-659-7 (paperback)
ISBN 978-963-386-660-3 (ebook)
ISSN 3004-1430 (print)

Library of Congress Cataloging-in-Publication Data

Names: Qvortrup, Matt, author.
Title: The political brain : the emergence of neuropolitics / Matt
Qvortrup.
Description: Budapest, Hungary ; New York, NY : Central European
University Press, 2024. | Series: Ceu press perspectives | Includes
bibliographical references and index.
Identifiers: LCCN 2024000884 (print) | LCCN 2024000885 (ebook)
ISBN 9789633866597 (paperback) | ISBN 9789633866603 (adobe pdf)
Subjects: LCSH: Political science—Philosophy. | Neurosciences—Political
aspects. | Neurosciences—Philosophy. | BISAC: POLITICAL SCIENCE /
Globalization
Classification: LCC JA71 .Q77 2024 (print) | LCC JA71 (ebook) | DDC
320.01/9—dc23/eng/20240214
LC record available at https://lccn.loc.gov/2024000884
LC ebook record available at https://lccn.loc.gov/2024000885

"All of our [belief] systems...communism, capitalism, religion, science...originated in electrochemical currents flowing through this three-pound lump of flesh encased in the skull."

Karl Ove Knausgård, "The Terrible Beauty of Brain Surgery"[1]

Contents

Foreword

Matt Qvortrup's book *The Political Brain: The Emergence of Neuropolitics* is an engaging and compelling read on the newly developing field of neuropolitics or understanding the brain, cognition, emotion and motivation of politicians and voters.

The book explains what we know on this topic to date, but also raises many questions and ethical and societal issues. Looking into the future, will voters demand that politicians participate not only in debates, but in functional magnetic resonance imaging (fMRI) studies to determine whether they are telling the truth or lying about their campaign pledges? As voters, we may have biases that we are unaware of or affirm statements because it may seem more socially acceptable to do so whether we agree with them or not. However, fMRI studies are able to detect these unconscious biases. Furthermore, neuropolitics can gain from experience in neuromarketing. fMRI studies in neuromarketing have shown that what we are willing to spend our money on is detected more accurately by the brain's reward system, including the ventral striatum, rather than our statement on questionnaires or surveys. This could in future be applied to political slogans, when our ventral striatum "lights up" or activates, that is the slogan that we like and would make us want to vote for that political party. We may even be able to detect when a swing voter is developing a strong allegiance to one particular political party by determining whether the brain's habit system is activated when viewing that party's logos.

The Political Brain also brings in references and discussion of historical and philosophical examples to provide insight into current behaviors by politicians and voters. Throughout time, there have always been in-groups and out-groups, those with whom you identify with and those with whom you do not. However, neuroimaging studies have identified that empathy while watching an ingroup. It turns out that being in pain yourself and seeing a member of your in-group in pain activates a very similar network in the brain. However, the activation in this network is strongly decreased if the person is not in your in-group. Fortunately, this reduced empathy can be changed. The brain signature and empathy can be increased through getting to know members and more familiarity with the out-group. This is strong evidence that exposure to ideas and people who differ from us can influence our brains and behavior. This sends an important message to members of opposite political parties: that interacting and understanding others' perspectives and opinions can be beneficial to establishing consensus on important decisions and promoting a flourishing society.

Important for all Governments is that our Leaders make good quality decisions under uncertainty and risk. This requires both good "cold" or rational decision-making, but also good "hot" or emotional and social decision-making. Hot or risky decisions are often time-limited. Neuroscientists know a great deal about the brain regions and networks involved in these two forms of decisions. For example, the dorsolateral prefrontal cortex is critical for cold planning and problem solving, while the ventromedial cortex and orbitofrontal cortex guide optimal risky decision-making. Political leaders with vision also need superior cognitive flexibility in addressing global challenges, such as climate change, renewable energy and food security.

Cognitive flexibility, which involves a fronto-striatal circuit in the brain, is necessary for switching to innovative solutions when attempts at old solutions have failed. Superimposed on the cold and hot circuitry in the brain are the neurotransmitters or chemicals, including dopamine, noradrenaline and serotonin, which modulate cognition, emotion and motivation. We know that there are cognitive enhancing drugs, such as modafinil, that reduce fatigue, improve cognitive flexibility and planning and problem solving and boost task-related motivation. With the further development in neuropolitics, there may be a time when the public expects our political leaders to use these cognitive enhancing drugs to counteract the effects on cognition of jet-lag and ageing brains or perhaps just to ensure that they are making the optimal possible decision.

Professor Barbara J Sahakian, PhD, DSc, FBA, FMedSci
University of Cambridge, Department of Psychiatry

Preface: The Brain in Political Research

"Never the twain shall meet." It used to be the case that neuroscience and political science were as far apart as the geographical poles in Rudyard Kipling's *The Ballad of East and West*.[2] But this has changed in recent years. What was once science fiction (readers might be familiar with Steven Spielberg's *Minority Report*, starring Tom Cruise and Max von Sydow) is now closer to becoming reality. Pioneering papers—many of which will be cited below—are able to literally "read" our minds and to distinguish between conservative and liberal brains, spot when we are dishonest, explain what happens in our brain when we succumb to hate speech, and a host of other things.

Hitherto, there have been scattered attempts by political scientists to use the brain—and some attempts by biologists to apply their knowledge to political subjects. This book will, above all, introduce this thinking to readers who are sympathetic to, but unfamiliar with, the brain and how neuroscience can elucidate our knowledge about politics.

This little book, by contrast, is rather different from other works in the field as it also explains how the ideas of political philosophy have a neurological correlate. In a sense, it provides a neuroscience perspective on political philosophy. Or, to put it differently, it looks at brain science through the prism of political theory. So, we shall, among other things, look at how the political psychology of Plato can be understood through fMRI-scans, and how the ideal of deliberation as developed by Aristotle can be understood and deepened through the same techniques.

Part of this book is based on research I undertook for the *BBC Radio4 Analysis Program*, entitled *The Political Brain*, which broadcast in 2023. I am grateful to my producer Bob Howard for asking probing questions and for forcing me to explain things that may not always be entirely obvious to those without training in neuroscience. I am also grateful to distinguished colleagues who have provided their input, including, among others, Professor Barbara Sahakian, Dr. Darren Schreiber, Professor Skyler Cranmer, and especially Dr. Liya Yu, whose book *Vulnerable Minds: The Neuropolitics of Divided Societies* prompted me to put my thoughts down on paper.[3] I am also indebted to Priscilla Afua Johnson who provided me with inspiration in proving the capacity of our brain to multitask and to focus on what is essential.

As in all cases, I alone bear the responsibility for the book—the good, the bad, and the downright incomprehensible.

Matt Qvortrup
Whale Beach, NSW, Australia
17th July 2023

Meiner Muse gewidmet

Introduction

The State of Neuropolitics

We have politics on our mind. Or, perhaps, more accurately, we have politics in many parts of the *cerebrum* (the Latin name for said organ). Until recently, political scientists—and indeed even psychologists and philosophers—failed to use neuroscience when dealing with political issues. Politics—in so far as it was measured—was understood through the prism of opinion polling and focus groups, and in some cases through the writings of old masters and political philosophers.

In many ways, it was odd that political scientists did not go back to the basics of decision-making and ask what causes us to make choices. Psychology would have been such an obvious choice for students of this discipline to use. After all, it is a behavioral science that deals with the motives for choosing one party over another. Yet, to use psychology you need to build on solid foundations. And these were not forthcoming. In academic psychology, Freud and his followers hypothesized the existence of a subconscious *id* in constant battle with the *superego* but never even sought to locate this in the brain,[4] and even more so, the aptly named behavioral psychologists looked at patterns of behavior and treated the mind as a "black box."[5] In the 1960s, of course, political science was largely synonymous with behaviorism, but looking at the micro-foundations of why we make decisions was never part of the equation, and this paradigm of political thinking was based more on the functionalist sociology of Talcott Parsons than on the operant conditioning psychology of Ivan Pavlov or B.F. Skinner.[6]

This didn't change much when political science turned towards rational choice analysis and institutionalism in the 1980s. It slightly puzzled me as a newcomer to the science of politics. Having originally started my academic journey in neuroscience, I was so obsessed with politics (and disappointed with brain science) that I transferred to politics (as this academic subject is called at Oxford) and eventually gained a doctorate in the latter field.

Yet, I was surprised to find that no references at all were made to biology in my new discipline. While I was fascinated by the rigor of the sophisticated models of electoral behavior, and even used them in my own research to forecast the outcomes of referendums, such as the "Brexit vote,"[7] I was never fully convinced by the claimed advances of the economic modeling in political science. Still, I was happy to use them and published articles that sought to explain such matters as terrorism and voting behavior using the narrow definition of human behavior used by economists. I did so on the premise, originally developed by Milton Friedman, that it is not the realism of the assumptions but the accuracy of the predictions that matter. As he put it:

> Truly important and significant hypotheses will be found to have "assumptions" that are wildly inaccurate descriptive representations of reality, and, in general, the more significant the theory, the more unrealistic the assumptions (in this sense). The reason is simple. A hypothesis is important if it "explains" much by little, that is, if it abstracts the common

and crucial elements from the mass of complex and detailed circumstances surrounding the phenomena to be explained and permits valid predictions on the basis of them alone.[8]

At the risk of providing a bit too much autobiography, I went on to analyze terrorism using this framework, and concluded that political violence is the result of weighing up of the costs and benefits of engaging in democratic politics or, alternatively, forcing yourself into the political system by, so to speak, blowing the door to it off its hinges.[9] My contention was that the more inclusive the political system (e.g., the more it allows minorities to participate through "consensus" institutions like proportional representation), the less likely we were to experience political violence.

Yet, when I lectured on the subject, people pointed out that the argument was oversimplified and that my "grievance theory" (the one just cited) was perhaps too neat, a bit too abstract, and just plain simplistic. My argument, as admirably summed up by a prominent critic, was that "political violence occurs when societal grievances do not find political expression and accommodation." However, the same critic found that I did not adequately demonstrate or prove an empirical relationship between consensus democracy and terrorism.[10] At the time, I stubbornly held to my position in public, but I had a lingering doubt about it in private, and quietly conceded the point. It is, I reflected, one thing to predict something mathematically or to even find a correlation; it is something entirely different to show a motive and to present a rounded theory.

What I personally found interesting—and secretly found mildly disturbing—was that the *rational choice* models work only *part* of the time. And perhaps, above all, that the "wildly inaccurate descriptive representations of reality"[11]—to quote Friedman—did not, and could often *not* be, justified by accurate predictions. Behaviorally, we are occasionally rational, and then sometimes we lose our proverbial marbles and act out of anger or on instinct. This line of reasoning was ultimately bordering on being banal, like the statement, "it rains except when it doesn't."

So, for this reason, I gradually and slowly began to return to neuroscience. This discipline, which I had followed only sporadically, had not stood still. My research, as presented here, is an attempt to (belatedly) respond to critics and to begin a new approach.

What I wanted to know was why and when we act rationally, and why we sometimes do the opposite. That is, not just answering a banal statement like, "Birds either fly or they don't," but to use the same metaphor to explain what prompts them to take flight, i.e., to identify the cause of them flying off. Hence, I figured that a truly new theory would be one that distinguished between (and explained) when we make a rational decision and when we do not.

Such distinctions, I was aware, had been proposed before in the history of political philosophy. For example, in his *Republic* (and later in the *Phaedrus*), Plato introduced a tripartite division of the soul. In his reading, it consisted of *thymos* (the emotional element) and *epithumia* (appetite and bodily desires in general), both of which were to be ruled over by *nous* (commonly, if somewhat inaccurately, translated "intellect").[12] But things have moved on since Plato. And as much as

I admired and idolized the great Greek sage, I wanted to bring his thinking up-to-date, or rather to complement it through the recent advances in neuroscience.

My ambition was (and is) to see if we could somehow combine the approaches of philosophy and neuroscience and find a place for rational choice as a subset of one of the behaviors. The aim of this short book, then, is to put Friedmanian rationality in its place, although not to abandon it, as it is still a valuable approach. Rather, the aim is to find out where and when it can be used, and to understand the biological as well as the philosophical aspects of human behavior. But overall, the ambition is to develop a new science of politics, a new paradigm that (in part at least) explains political behavior through an understanding of the brain.

All this may be rather ambitious. It is. And why not? Why waste the readers' time spouting platitudes when you can put forward a new paradigm of doing politics. All this, I should add, is nothing totally new. To be sure, few if any have combined neuropolitics (I will explain the term below) with philosophy. Much as this may sound new to many readers, there are, in fact, several studies that look at the neurobiological bases of our political behavior.[13] And not just new ones, I might add.

This little book, then, has not invented the study of politics through brain science and neurology. But then again, Thomas Hobbes did not invent the mechanistic view of the world; he merely applied this model to create a new synthesis. Likewise, David Hume did not invent Newtonian physics, but what the Scottish philosopher did was to "introduce the experimental Method of Reasoning into Moral Subjects."[14]

So, what I am modestly doing is to introduce the neuro-scientific method into political philosophy and into empirical political science. How, then, is this possible? The main answer to that is that we now have so-called fMRI scans, which allow us to indirectly see what goes on in the mind when we are presented with different facts or images or performing different tasks. In chapter one below, I shall explain (hopefully in a pedagogical way) how all this works.

Why is this important? Well, for starters, one of the things these developments and these advances in neuroscience allow us to do is to put Hobbes, Spinoza, Aristotle, and Plato in the fMRI-Scanner and see what goes on in our brains when we are exposed to extreme (and mundane) political statements.

As I was researching this, it seemed that others had already been thinking along the same lines. One writer noted, "naturally, there is no shortage of studies about the brain and its political inclinations. And it seems that liberals have a slightly larger anterior cingulate cortex (the part of the frontal cortex above the corpus callosum), while conservatives allegedly have an atrophied right amygdala."[15] On a personal level, I was excited to see this. When I took up political science in the early 1990s, these methods were yet to be developed. They are now. And this has radical implications for the way we see and do political analysis. As it turned out, the reference to "no shortage of studies" is somewhat overcooked, and there is a relative paucity of studies—at least at the time of writing—that cover brain politics.

But all great things start with small beginnings, Rome was not built in a day, and so on. As already noted, this book is not the first to use these approaches to study political attitudes and behaviors. And there is, despite the relative dearth of studies, already something to build on—just as there was something on which Hume could base his *Treatise*. In a recent review article (albeit one written in a slightly forbidding language), the authors sum up the advances in the following words, in a section that deserves to be quoted at length:

> The emerging interdisciplinary field of political neuroscience (or neuropolitics) is focused on understanding the neural mechanisms underlying political information processing and decision making. ... This includes brain regions involved in affective and evaluative processing, such as the amygdala, insula, anterior cingulate, and orbitofrontal cortex, as well as regions involved in social cognition (e.g., medial prefrontal cortex [PFC]), decision making (e.g., dorsolateral PFC), and reward processing (e.g., ventral striatum). Existing research in political neuroscience has largely focused on understanding candidate evaluation, political participation, and ideological differences. ...While the field is still relatively new, this work has begun to improve our understanding of how people engage in motivated reasoning about political candidates and elected officials and the extent to which these processes may be automatic versus relatively more controlled. Other work has focused on understanding how brain differences are related to differences in political opinion, showing both structural and functional variation between political liberals and political conservatives.[16]

I am aware that these references to neuroanatomy may seem bewildering and confusing to those who have not sat through anatomy lectures at medical school. Hence, in this book, we shall proceed step-by-step. And it is important to stress that there is still some way to go. And, yet, advances have been made. As Liya Yu has written, "Although this field is still at its infancy, and therefore a comprehensive incorporation of social brain data at the research and teaching level has yet to fully materialize within political science, a new biological turn has slowly but steadily taken place within the social sciences."[17]

The chapters are as follows. In Chapter One, entitled *The Brain: A Philosophical and Historical Introduction*, we will provide an overview of what we know about the brain, the history of this knowledge (how we got to where we are today), and how all this relates to what philosophers have written about the subject before. This chapter will also summarize the basics of the microbiology of the brain, synapses, neurotransmitters, basic anatomy, and so on. The chapter will, moreover, show how advances have already been made, which allow us to use neuroimaging to detect when people lie (fMRI scans have been used in criminal cases in India). In addition, we will see how, using this technology, we can literally see what is in our mind's eye.

Following this, in Chapter Two, entitled *The Neuropolitics of Us and Them*, we look at how the use of brain imaging can help us understand the polarization in society. The main argument in the chapter is that we can combine Plato's tripartite division of the brain to understand when we act angrily and when we are more inclusive. The chapter will introduce the main model and then move on to empirical examples of the differences between "globalists" and "nativists"—or what former British Prime Minister Theresa May called "anywheres" and "somewheres." In addition to this, the chapter will—as a kind of excursus—provide a case study of the neuropolitics of rebellion and revolution and try to explain political uprisings—like the attacks on the US Congress in January 2021—based on our understanding of neurological processes.

In Chapter Three, *Social Neuroscience, Political Attitudes, and Election Campaigns*, we look at the differences between conservative and liberal brains. We consider if neuropolitics can be used to identify the ideological outlook of individual voters and what these reveals about them. For example, we ask whether one side of politics is more empathetic than others and whether conservatives are more likely to be driven by emotions (especially anger) than liberal electors. We also look at how we might be able to use neuropolitics to predict (or at least understand) the outcome of elections. This part of the chapter is mainly focused on neuropolitics as a method for influencing voters. It introduces what we know about political advertising and the work that political consultants have done throughout history, and then contrasts this with what we may be able to do with the help of fMRI scans and other methods. This chapter will also look at why some people have a "taste" for different kinds of politics.

So far, the chapters have been of a more descriptive nature; this changes in Chapter Four. Entitled *The Listening Brain: The State We Ought to Be In*, the chapter shows how we can enhance democracies through neuropolitics and how we, by means of this, can get a step closer to mending our fractured societies. In particular, the chapter shows how Aristotle's concept of deliberation can be understood through fMRI scans, and how this knowledge can become the basis for a new political theory, or, to paraphrase Hume, neuropolitics may literally introduce science into a moral subject.[18]

As per usual, the book is rounded off with a summary of the findings and several avenues for readers to take to get deeper into the subject. In the epilogue, it will be suggested that neuropolitics potentially provides the outlines of a paradigm shift in the sense presented by Thomas S. Kuhn, namely, as a completely new approach to studying a subject that solves the problems that earlier theories (e.g., rational choice and behaviorism) *could solve*, as well as the "anomalies" these theories could not solve. As such, neuropolitics is, potentially, a revolutionary departure. This might be a bold claim, and you might be skeptical at this stage, but bear with me and hear me out. Perhaps, when you have read this little book, you too will be a convert, or at least more open to a new and literally scientific way of analyzing politics.

Chapter One

The Brain: A Philosophical and Historical Introduction

To introduce a subject as complicated as neuropolitics to novices who, while they may be well read in economics, philosophy, and political science, are unlikely to have much of an understanding of, let alone knowledge about, neurobiology, is a tall order. It is like putting the cart before the horse to write about findings before we have introduced the concepts, and yet it can be tedious to begin with the mundane parts. But a bit of history might, I hope, whet the appetite.

Neuropolitics, in a sense, deals with an issue that has exercised minds for millennia, though in different ways. Those interested in politics—and philosophy and theology—have always been puzzled by what drives us and why we make decisions. This pondering led to the birth of philosophy. Over 2000 years ago, the philosopher Plato (427–348 BCE) said that our minds were divided into reason and anger. When we feel "left behind," he argued, we are prone to anger and irrational behavior. Thus, democracies broke down because the citizens demanded ever more recognition and rose up because they perceived they were not given—what they themselves considered to be—their due respect. Under these circumstances, they would often puzzlingly undercut their own freedoms by electing an autocrat who claimed to speak on their behalf. Angry that they have been left out, the political system would become polarized, and Plato wrote, "hence arise impeachments, prosecutions, and trials, directed by each party against the other," and before long the people will "select a special champion of their cause, whom they maintain and exalt to greatness."[19] All of this had to do with *thymos*. When a man or woman feels that someone "has been unjust to him [or her]," the spirit within them starts "boiling" and she or he will "[fight] for what this individual believes to be just."[20]

Put simply, what neuropolitics aims to do is show how this mechanism works neurologically and to discover what scanning the brain can reveal about our political affiliations, including the angry voters who opt for a tyrant. Though, of course, neuropolitics also does other things. Indeed, as we shall see, brain responses might even be used to determine which policies we might find attractive. And we are not—as we shall see shortly—far from a situation in which we can use brain scans to predict elections, or certainly, to reveal the ideological position of the voter in a brain scanner. Science fiction? Scary? Fascinating? Take your pick, but this is the reality whatever you may think of it!

To write about the brain and decisions is likely to open a hornet's nest of controversy. In the history of philosophy and science, there has always been an argument concerning the ontological status of our mind.

The father of medicine, Hippocrates (460–370 BCE), was of the opinion that we were basically just biology. "Men [and presumably women and non-binary] ought to know that from the brain, and the brain only, arise our pleasures, joys, laughter, and jests, as well as our sorrows, pains, griefs, and tears."[21]

Interestingly, the same view was taken in the Old Testament. The ancient Hebrews did not believe in an immaterial soul. And, historically speaking, one of the challenges the high priests in the New Testament faced from Jesus Christ was that the self-proclaimed "Son of Man" preached that we do have a soul and an afterlife, even when our brains have ceased to work.[22]

Some philosophers, most notably René Descartes (1596–1650), famously claimed that we were a mixture of body and soul, respectively *res extensa* and *res cogitans*.[23] For other philosophers, the situation was even more pronounced. While Benedict de Spinoza (1632–1677) was sympathetic towards a materialistic interpretation, in his *Ethics* he was convinced that "mind and body are one and the same." He also acknowledged that—at least at the time—"no one knows how or by what means the mind moves the body."[24] John Locke (1632–1704) dabbled in medicine, but he too was skeptical as regards the possibility of understanding the brain as a machine, as was first suggested by the Danish scientist (and later Catholic priest) Niels Steensen/Nicolaus Steno (1638–1686).[25] Locke's famous *Essay Concerning Human Understanding* struck an even more downcast prediction as to what we can know about the neurobiological side of the mind, writing that "we have the ideas of matter and thinking, but possibly shall never be able to know whether any mere material thinks or no."[26]

While there were thinkers in subsequent centuries who espoused a muscular materialism, it was not until the last decade of the twentieth century that we were able to (indirectly) associate brain activity with thoughts and tasks. Thanks to so-called fMRI scans, we can see what goes on in our heads when we think about politics.

The brain is a complex organ. There are a number of things that need to be nipped in the bud before we start. First of all, there is the issue of so-called *localism*. In the nineteenth century, when researchers began to study the brain in earnest, the discipline of phrenology was much talked about. The German physician Franz Joseph Gall (1758–1828) proposed that certain parts of the brain were responsible for certain predispositions. These tendencies could be measured by the shape of the skull. So, based on the bumps on a person's head you could—so he argued—determine their personality. Herman Melville referred to it as a credible theory in his famous novel *Moby Dick; or, The Whale*. When discussing the Pacific Islander, Queequeg, he noted that

> his head was phrenologically an excellent one. It may seem ridiculous, but it reminded me of General Washington's head, as seen in the popular busts of him. It had the same long regularly graded retreating slope from above the brows, which were likewise very projecting, like two long promontories thickly wooded on top. Queequeg was George Washington cannibalistically developed.[27]

But even among scientists—or rather, especially among them—there was widespread skepticism about this theory. At the time when Queen Victoria had her grandchildren's craniums checked,[28] time was already running out for phrenology. More experimental neuroscientists were looking at the microlevels of the brain to understand how it worked. This led, first of all, to some rather remarkable images of brain cells—or neurons, as they soon became known.

But before we get to that, we ought to mention the curious case of Phineas Gage. He was a railway worker who was hit by a long iron pole while supervising an explosion. It penetrated his skull through the eye and shot up through the frontal lobes. Miraculously, Gage survived but his behavior changed. Previously, he had been courteous and polite. After the accident, a physician who examined him reported that he was "fitful, irreverent, indulging at times in the grossest profanity (which was not previously his custom), manifesting but little deference for his fellows, impatient of restraint or advice when it conflicts with his desires.... A child in his intellectual capacity and manifestations, he has the animal passions of a strong man."[29] What the case of Gage showed was that issues to do with self-restraint and social intelligence (or the lack thereof) are associated with exactly those parts of the frontal lobes that were destroyed. Gage survived because the accident only affected parts of the brain associated with cognitive functions—none of the ones that have to do with, say, the heart, digestion, endocrinological secretion, etc. He is now mentioned in pretty much every book published on neuropsychology because his case proved that certain parts of the brain are activated when we engage in social behavior.

At the time when this was happening, neuroanatomists were at work in the field of microbiology. This was to have a major impact in the field, though not immediately. The first, and rather beautiful, images of neurons were produced in 1873 by the Italian scientist Camilio Golgi (1843–1926), who used silver staining to visualize what neurons look like. However, Golgi did not think that neurons by themselves were all that important. At the time, many believed that the brain was one large bundle. This, by the way, was called the *reticular theory*. Experimental work by the Spanish histologist (an expert on tissue) Santiago Ramón y Cajal (1852–1934) led to the development of the *neuron theory*. Looking at the brain cells of birds, Cajal showed that these were not all connected and that they were not all bundled together. The two men, Cajal and Golgi, disagreed but were both awarded the Nobel Prize for medicine in the same year, 1906. But it took until the mid-1950s to prove Cajal right. This conclusion was due in part to the invention of the electron microscope but also to studies of traumatized brains.

Neurons and synapses: The chemistry of thought and drugs

The adult brain is made up of about eighty-six billion cells called neurons. They differ in size from 4 to 100 microns. They all have the same shape and function in the same way. When we think—or do any other cerebral activity—a neuron fires a neurotransmitter from one end called the axon. This enters the gap between nerve cells (called the synapse) and is received by the so-called *dendrite* of another neuron.

So, how does this work? A modicum of elementary chemistry is needed, which might require a bit of concentration. Basically, the inside of the neuron is negatively charged with chloride atoms. When a neuron is activated, its membrane is opened and positively charged sodium atoms enter the brain cell. This leads to a chain reaction, which ultimately leads to the end of the neuron. Once the reaction gets there, neuro-transmitters stored in small pockets (called *vesicles*) are re-leased and find their way into the synapse, where they are then received by another neuron.

So, the key to any brain activity, then, are neurotransmit-ters, of which there are about 100. Some of the better known are *serotonin* and *dopamine*. The former is associated with sex, sleep, and crucially for the purposes of this book, "serotonin is positively correlated with sensitivity to social factors and modulates social behavior in a 'for-better-and-for-worse' manner."[30] The latter is associated with motor control and rewards. Significantly, a reduction in *dopamine* is responsible for many of the symptoms of Parkinson's disease. Addition-ally, and once again, more importantly for our purposes, a feeling and even an anticipation of rewards increases the level of this neurotransmitter in the brain.[31] Without going into this in detail, many class A drugs work by effecting dopamine levels in the brain. Thus, cocaine gets its effect by blocking the removal of *dopamine* from the synapse.

Much as the idea of *localism* had been discredited during the age of phrenology, many experiments continued to show that certain areas—albeit in interaction with others—were responsible for patterns of behavior. For example, in an often-cited study, the English-born Canadian psychologist Brenda Milner carried out experiments on patient H. M., who had had his hippocampus removed because of a botched lobotomy. As a result of this, he had no short-term memory. What was crucial about this was that the complete lack of this part of the brain meant that localism still plays a role, though only in connection with other parts of the brain. This was an important finding, one that basically laid the basis for the present paradigm of neuroscience.[32]

Thus, focusing on parts of the brain, as Milner did—albeit in interaction with other parts—allows us to predict beliefs and behaviors. This is a novel revolutionary development, though one that is yet to be fully appreciated and utilized in political thinking. But we need to be mindful of the nuances for fear of being accused of sensationalism.

So, let's get back to the fundamentals. The brain is not simply divided into areas that are responsible for specific tasks or thoughts. Several areas have many functions. And it is oversimplifying that a center such as the *amygdala* (an evolutionarily old part of the mid-brain) is the fight and flight center. But, at the same time, this part of the brain is associated with these feelings, actions, and emotions. So, as a shorthand—and as a necessary simplification—activation of this center shows us something. For example, as we shall see, activation of this part of the brain is more pronounced in supporters of populist voters, those whose motivation for engaging in politics is fear and hate. (We shall return to this in the next chapter.)

But to be scientifically accurate, we should talk about connectivity with some areas playing a larger role than others. As a study pointed out,

> The human brain is characterized by structural and functional connectivity within and between regions. Structural connectivity refers to the anatomical organization of the brain by means of fiber tracts. Recent advances in magnetic resonance imaging (MRI) and image processing provide various

means to quantify structural connectivity in a non-invasive way using short-range local measures and/or long-range tract tracing procedures, called diffusion tractography. Functional connectivity refers to statistical dependence between time series of electro-physiological activity and (de)oxygenated blood levels in distinct regions of the brain.[33]

If you want to put a name of a scientist to this paradigm, it would be the Russian neuroscientist Alexander Luria (1902–1977). He was the author of a much-cited, and rather well-written, book called *The Working Brain*.[34] This study presented the now prevailing theory that different areas are specialized to carry out particular roles, but with the important twist that these specialized areas are not sufficient on their own to produce a function (e.g., language). Integration is required for thoughts to occur, as "different brain modules act in an interdependent manner in much the same way that a complete symphony is dependent upon the coordinated performance of different sections of an orchestra."[35]

So, brain science has moved on since the localism of Gall (see above). But it is still the case that certain functions are mainly associated with a particular part of the brain, and we can see this on fMRI scans. Overall, then, the *functional systems model* states that the unit of receiving and analyzing information relates to different areas of the cerebrum, such as the occipital lobe (vision), the temporal lobe (inter alia auditory functions), and the parietal lobe (tactile sensation), and that these are transmitted to the frontal lobes (cognitive and executive functions) for analysis and assessment. For Luria, then, it was clear that the prefrontal lobes perform a superior role as "a superstructure above all other parts of the cerebral cortex, so that they perform a far more universal function of general regulation of behaviour."[36]

So, what matters are the functional relations between, say, the amygdala (which is activated when we are scared) and the part of the prefrontal cortex that is associated with, among other things, planning and decision-making. This is where it gets exciting because not all people show the same reaction. Some people, those of a conservative persuasion, will have re-actions that differ from those of a more liberal outlook. All this can be seen on brain scans and can also be inferred from surveys. But we are getting ahead of ourselves, and we will get back to this in the next chapters.

So where are we up to as regards our ability to read other people's minds for clues as to their politics? What do we know? Let's take a step back and consider this from a philosophical perspective.[37] In the history of philosophy, the great thinkers talked about our "ideas," about those things that are private to us. In the words of the English empirical philosopher John Locke, the idea "stands for whatsoever is the Object of the Understanding, when a man thinks."[38] For him, as well as for the philosophers who came after him, these were private. You didn't need to be a canonical philosopher to conclude this. In folklore, it has long been recognized that while we cannot speak publicly, at least we can have our thoughts to ourselves. *Die Gedanken sind frei* is a famous German folk song originally from the thirteenth century. In the English-speaking world, it was brought to a wider audience by the folksinger Pete Seeger, who sang:

> My thoughts give me power
> No scholar can map them
> No hunter can trap them[39]

Well, the authors of the folk song and the liberal American troubadour lived and worked before the emergence of fMRI scans. But now, quite literally, we can get a picture of the images before our mind's eye. Enter Steve Martin. Not, mind you, because the famous silver-haired comedian himself got involved in research. He didn't, though his colleague Colin Firth (he of *The King's Speech* fame) did.[40]

Admittedly, for those who read the abstract of the study, it wasn't at first apparent what Mr. Martin had to do with it. The neuroscientist Jack Gallant and his colleagues from the University of California, Berkeley, who carried out the experiment, reported:

> We recorded BOLD [blood oxygen level-dependent) signals in occipitotemporal area visual cortex of human subjects who watched natural movies and fit the model separately to individual voxels. Visualization of the fit models reveals how early visual areas represent the information in movies. To demonstrate the power of our approach, we also constructed a Bayesian decoder by combining estimated encoding models with a sampled natural movie prior. The decoder provides remarkable reconstructions of the viewed movies. These results demonstrate that dynamic brain activity measured under naturalistic conditions can be decoded using current fMRI technology.[41]

So, what about Steve Martin?—I hear you ask impatiently. Why mention him at all? Because he was featured in the "natural movies." This is what happened. Three subjects (not a large sample, admittedly) were shown short video clips of the actor while their brains were scanned. The activity in the occipital part of the brain (that which deals with vision) was then electronically transmitted to a computer, which used the information to come up with an image of the actor, albeit a blurred one. In addition to the film clip with Mr. Martin, the respondents were also shown a video clip of elephants roaming in the wild. These were also transmitted to the computer, which generated tolerable representations of the animals in the wild. In other words, the researchers were literally able to make representations of the mind's inner eye.

The media reported the findings with a bit of hype that was probably a bit over the top. The *Daily Mail*, not normally a source for serious writing on neuroscience, reported that there was a brain scanner capable of "reading" people's dreams accurately enough to see what they were dreaming about—a claim that somewhat overegged the proverbial pudding.[42] But the findings don't need to be hyped to be indicative of how far we have come.

Once again, what does this mean in practice? Quite a lot, in fact. One way in which such findings could prove useful is in police detection and in the courts. In fact, there are some indications that brain scans may replace lie detectors in the long run. This, at least, is what Barbara Sahakian, a professor of neuropsychology at the University of Cambridge, believes. She cited pioneering work by Dr. Giorgio Ganis, a neuroscience specialist at Plymouth University,[43] and Daniel Langleben, a pioneer of fMRI scanning now at the University of Pennsylvania:[44]

When Daniel Langleben first did some studies on whether you could tell whether somebody was lying or not in an F MRI scanner, he used a model and it was only about 77% accurate at spotting a lie, so that wasn't really much better than a polygraph. But then that model was used by a company and they developed the model more and they were able to increase the accuracy to about 89%. And there's actually a study by Giorgio Ganis.[45] What they did was to ask about birth dates and because they used autobiographical material rather than sort of more artificial material, his model actually achieved 100% accuracy, so it might well be that you can detect lying in a scanner very accurately.[46]

Ok, so you may not be quite convinced yet. Admittedly, there is a long way from telling if someone is lying about their date of birth to whether they're telling the truth about, say, a crime they have committed. Well, once again, prepare to be surprised.

Neurotechnology of this kind has been monetized by a company called *No Lie MRI*. The company has quite openly sought to develop fMRI scans to further the development of a new generation of polygraphs. The idea may seem like science fiction. What they have effectively done is put defendants under a scanner to see if they are telling the truth. Some believe that this use of neuroscience has the potential to change the legal system.[47] Is this true? To be sure, this approach has been criticized. For example, Pardo and Patterson have suggested that the approach is too reductionist.[48] Yet, these criticisms at the more philosophical level have to be set against more pragmatic and partial studies that show that we can detect— and even forecast—criminal behavior based on brain scans.

Moreover, the difficulties that may exist with the technology are not a sufficient reason for criticizing the approach more fundamentally. In the mid-1970s, the American Psychological Association officially concluded that "psychologists are not competent to make such judgments."[49]

Thankfully, the above is no longer the case. Psychology is now often used in criminal cases. Since the 1993 United States Supreme Court case *Daubert v. Merrell Dow Pharmaceuticals, Inc.*, the US federal standard for the admissibility of psychological profiles has been accepted. This role has been further expanded to include neuropsychology and has been refined in subsequent circuit court and Supreme Court decisions, in particular, the 1999 *Kumho Tire v. Carmichael Supreme Court* decision.[50]

So why not also use fMRI scans? Some people in America have reservations. Not so in India, where *neuroscientific evidence* (some call it neurolaw) has been used in real criminal trials. Thus, a woman who was accused of poisoning her ex-fiancée was put under a scanner and was convicted after an EEG examination using a slightly less sophisticated technique—one that utilizes the electronic activity of the brain.[51] In America, findings based on a similar use of technology—in this case, fMRI scans—were ruled inadmissible by the courts.[52] Needless to say, there are ethical concerns. For example,

> the possibility of predicting dangerousness via neurobiological markers raises a number of ethical and legal issues concerned with potential violations of specific offenders' individual rights and civil liberties. These issues include

the potential discrimination and stigmatization of offenders based on their 'neurobiological profile', procedural and constitutional rights violations (e.g. violation of the privilege against self-incrimination), and criminal policy matters (e.g. the dividing line between criminal responsibility and social dangerousness).

However, the same writer also hints that these might be overcome.[53] Further, should we not use all our knowledge to obtain a just outcome in a criminal trial? Should there be barriers to the truth in matters that concern violations of our personal security and even our lives? A strong case could certainly be made for the view expressed by Glenn and Raine that if neurobiological markers can reliably boost the accuracy of criminal behavior predictions, "it could be viewed as ethically questionable not to use such knowledge."[54] Overall, Sahakian and Gottwald find that that "the evidence is encouraging and advancements of [neuro]science will certainly lead to the development of more reliable and accurate lie-detection techniques."[55]

You may have your own opinion. And it may be related to your personal political views. So, this discussion is for a longer study. Suffice it to say, however, that the prospects of predicting criminal behavior are no longer pure science fiction.

But how does it work? Old-fashioned lie detectors focused on spotting an untruth. So, which part of the brain gets activated when we tell fibs? To put it in slightly simplified, though still accurate, terms, lying was associated with both the anterior cingulate gyrus (located at the bottom of the central *sulcus* that separates the two brain hemispheres) and the ventrolateral prefrontal cortex. The latter is interesting as this part of the brain (at the bottom of the frontal lobe) is associated with inhibition and risk averseness. The former is interesting too, as the anterior cingulate gyrus is associated with motivation, decision-making, and cost-benefit calculation. So, when we lie—which, to be honest (sic!) we all do to varying degrees—we employ a strategy of risk averseness (we are afraid of being caught) as we weigh up the cost-benefit of telling a fib.[56]

What all the above amounts to is more than neuroanatomy. What these results show is that our thoughts are no longer private. *Liberae sunt nostrae cogitationes* (Free are our thoughts) wrote Cicero in *Pro Milone*, one of his most famous speeches. As a defense lawyer (but perhaps not later as a politician), the Roman would have been concerned that prosecutors in India have used fMRI scans to determine if defendants are telling the truth. Though, as a clever politician and debater, he is sure to have found weak spots in the argument. The study that showed that we can detect lies in the brain with greater accuracy than polygraphs was, in fact, funded by the aforementioned *No Lie MRI*.[57] And that is no lie! There is, however, no reason to believe that this peer-reviewed article was biased or based on flawed evidence. The most likely conclusion Cicero would have drawn, had he been honest with himself, would probably have been *Liberae non sunt nostrae cogitationes*, that "thoughts are not free."

We could cite other studies, but this is neither the time nor the place for a comprehensive literature review. The aim of this chapter was merely to provide a *tour d'horizon* of the state of the neuroscience art. Based on this necessarily brief overview, we can go on to look at how these insights can be used in the realm of politics.

Chapter Two

The Neuropolitics of Us and Them

Those who guide this people are leading them astray,
and those who are guided by them are swallowed up
Isaiah 9:16

In an unfortunate turn of phrase, the former British Prime Minister Theresa May made a distinction between "Anywheres" and "Somewheres."[58] In an uncharacteristic pandering to the darker elements of the "nasty party" (to use her own phrase from a decade and a half before), she drew attention to "us" and "them" and sought to utilize the appeal of singling out the "other." Finding a scapegoat is a tried and tested trick among politicians. And there are many politicians who are more guilty of succumbing to this than this otherwise tolerant and principled British politician. Whatever one thinks of such tactics, the aim here is to understand rather than condemn. And the fact that these antics seem to work electorally begs the question why? Besides sociological reasons why such tactics may work, relative deprivation and other theories come to mind.[59]

The question before us in this book is whether there is a neuropolitical or social neuroscientific explanation for the apparent efficacy of these tactics. The research to date shows clear indications that these strategies are effective because they appeal to some of the basest—and arguably oldest—parts of our brains. A couple of studies deserve to be singled out to give a sense of the state-of-the-art research.

In a pioneering study, Elizabeth Phelps and colleagues conducted an *Implicit Association Test (IAT)* and then triangulated the results with findings from fMRI scans. An IAT, in case you haven't heard about one before, is a psychological test where you are asked a number of questions that measure your unconscious bias towards other (typically vulnerable) groups. In other words, it is a measure of what you "really" think in your heart of hearts. What Phelps was interested in was whether it was possible to measure this implicit racism in the activation of the amygdala, a "subcortical structure known to play a role in emotional learning and evaluation."[60] The findings go some way in explaining implicit racism. Thus, Phelps and colleagues found that when White American subjects were presented with faces of unfamiliar Black and White males, "the strength of amygdala activation to Black-versus-White faces was correlated with two indirect (unconscious) measures of race evaluation (Implicit Association Test [IAT] and potentiated startle), but not with the direct (conscious) expression of race attitudes."[61]

That there is a correlation between our unconscious racism and the faces of another racial group is depressing, but there might be a silver lining, as the researchers also found that this correlation was only there if the faces were of unknown people. When shown images of well-known faces (e.g., Black celebrities), there was no such correlation. Thus, "these patterns were not obtained when the stimulus faces belonged to familiar and positively regarded Black and White individuals."[62] Whether this provides any comfort is an open question. It is certainly a positive that the White subjects were able to humanize the other if they knew him, her, or them. Yet, if we look at it from a social neuroscience perspective, the findings "suggest that amygdala and behavioural responses to Black-versus-White faces in White subjects reflect cultural evaluations of social groups modified by individual experience."[63]

So, it seems clear that feelings associated with "the other" are positively correlated with certain brain areas, or *regions of interest* (ROIs), as the jargon expresses it.[64] These findings chime with earlier research that shows—or, at the very least, indicates—that far-right extremism is associated with neural activity in the amygdala.[65] So, given that the amygdala is the part of the brain responsible for fight and flight, could this be the key to understanding the appeal of far-right rhetoric? And, indeed, might the activation of this part of the so-called *limbic system* more generally explain the salience of the targeting of "the other"?

To answer all this, we need to acknowledge that biology is "not deterministic" but conditional. That is, certain people have a particular disposition and others do not.[66] Whether genetically based or as a result of social factors, what we need to identify are the conditionals: the factors that prompt certain individuals to be susceptible to hate speech. One possibility is that our behavior—and the neural activity that goes with it—is a result of a genetic reason. In fact, there is some interesting research that points in that direction. Thus, some people with certain genetic dispositions are more likely to react in a particular way if this gene is triggered by external factors.[67] Other research, however, suggests that socioeconomic factors can prompt what has been referred to as "motivated social cognition."[68]

How does this work? Any sociological or political science explanation must be open to the potentially beneficial effects of creating a sense of belonging as a mechanism for achieving greater cohesion. Hence, we can hypothesize that having an ideology of "us" and "them"—or "Anywheres" and "Somewheres"—has often been seen as sociologically beneficial because it "brings people together, giving them an edge over those who lack this social glue."[69] In line with this, research by John Jost and colleagues is a case in point. Their study assumes that "conservative ideology should be more appealing to individuals who are either temporarily or chronically high in needs to manage uncertainty and threat."[70] So, could it be that those who live in "red states" (or the deprived areas of Britain that were termed the "red wall seats") who are little exposed to globalization (and hence to people of a different ethnicity or background) are more likely to display these traits?

We do not have direct evidence from Britain, but a study of Chinese and American research subjects displays some rather interesting findings. In an article with the telling title "Do You Feel My Pain?" Xiaojing Xu and colleagues[71] showed that when Chinese and Caucasian research subjects were shown film clips of compatriots and Caucasians, respectively, they only showed a response in the anterior cingulate cortex and insula (two areas associated with empathy) when pain was inflicted on people of their own ethnicity; the pain of strangers, however, left them cold.[72] In the words of the study:

> Perception of painful stimulation applied to faces increased activity in parts (e.g., ACC and frontal/insula cortex) of the neural circuits underlying first-person pain experience....

More interestingly, we found neuroimaging evidence for mod-
ulation of empathic neural responses by racial group membership, i.e., ACC empathic responses to perception of others in
pain decreased remarkably when participants viewed faces
of racial in-group members relative to racial out-group members. This effect was comparable in Caucasian and Chinese
subjects and suggests that modulations of empathic neural
responses by racial group membership are similar in different
ethnic groups.[73]

Now, this finding could perhaps lead to fatalism and resigna-
tion, as a kind of proof that there is nothing we can really do
and that we are destined to feel a lack of empathy towards "the
other." However, a follow-up study showed something else—
something altogether more encouraging, namely, that research
subjects who had lived extensive periods abroad had developed
(or learned) empathy towards those of a different racial and
ethnic background and became more empathetic. Thus, in the
article "Cultural Experiences Reduce Racial Bias in Neural
Responses to Others' Suffering," two of the same researchers
who had carried out the "Do You Feel My Pain" study found
something altogether less xenophobic. As the authors explain:

Using functional magnetic resonance imaging, we scanned
20 Chinese adults who were brought up in Western countries
(United States, United Kingdom, and Canada) where Caucasians consist of the majority of population....We found that
the neural activity in the pain matrix including the anterior
cingulate cortex, anterior insula, inferior frontal cortex and
somatosensory cortex was significantly increased in response
to painful versus non-painful stimuli applied to both Asian
and Caucasian models. Moreover, these empathic neural
responses to Asian and Caucasian models did not differ significantly and were positively correlated with each other.[74]

The conclusion that the researchers drew was that "cultural experiences with racial out-group members may increase the neural responses to the suffering of other-race individuals and thus reduce the racial bias in empathy."[75] As the researchers pointed out:

> These results were different from the previous work that showed significantly reduced empathic neural responses in the ACC and sensorimotor cortex to other-race than same-race faces. In particular, Chinese participants … showed reduced empathic neural responses to Caucasian than Chinese faces in the ACC. Therefore, unlike the Chinese participants in the previous studies, Chinese participants in the current work showed comparable empathic neural responses to the suffering of both same-race and other-race individuals and thus failed to show racial bias in empathic neural responses to the suffering of others.[76]

Now, of course, one single follow-up study does not prove that people become more empathetic when they become "Anywheres." However, the conclusion drawn by the study of the "Chinese globalists" (they had all studied in Australia) is rendered plausible by a similar study which reached the same conclusion.[77] For example, in "Racial Bias in Neural Response to Others' Pain is Reduced with Other-Race Contact," Yuan Cao and colleagues investigated whether exposure to other races would lead to growing empathy over time. In the study, they recruited Chinese subjects who had been in Australia between six months and five years. They found that there was a correlation between the time spent abroad and empathy towards Caucasians' perceived pain. The researchers found that:

Activation in the anterior cingulate to pain in other races increased significantly with the level of contact participants reported with people of the other race. Importantly, this correlation did not depend on the closeness of contact or personal relationships, but simply on the overall level of experience with people of the other race in their every-day environment. Racial bias in neural responses to others' pain, as a neural marker of empathy, therefore, changes with experience in new immigrants at least within 5 years of arrival in the new society and, crucially, depends on the level of contact with people of the other race in every-day life contexts.[78]

So, basically, we become more empathetic when we are exposed to others who are unlike ourselves. Maybe this is nothing new; indeed, René Descartes was on to the same thing when he wrote that "it is well to know something about the manners of different peoples, in order to form a sounder judgement of our own, and not to think everything contrary to our own ways absurd and irrational, as people usually do when they have never seen anything else."[79] What the philosopher knew from experience is something that we can now more or less directly see in fMRI scans.

Insurrections and neuropolitics

We are all the product of six million or so years of human evolution. All humans have a brain. It is important that we keep this in mind when we use neuroscience to understand social phenomena. Neuropolitics is—and should be—a means to understand and humanize the brains of opponents. We shall return to this in the last chapter of this book. But it is important to keep this in mind when we analyze political phenomena that relate to one side of politics, such as uprisings by far-right groups. These groups, whether in Germany in the 1930s or in America in January 2021, are often driven by the politics of "us and them," and sometimes result in dehumanization. We know this from several studies using neuropolitical approaches.[80] This is not only something we can see in the ubiquitous culture wars of the first half of the twenty-first century. It has been on display in the uprisings and riots that have taken place throughout time.

Since the dawn of politics, writers, philosophers, and practitioners have written about revolutions and rebellions. Way back in Ancient Rome, the historian (and one-time politician) Sallust, or Gaius Sallustius Crispus (86–35 BCE), penned his book *Bellum Catilinae*, usually translated as *The War Against Catiline*. His was a chronicle about an attempt to overthrow the Roman Republic—and an attempt to explain the underlying logic of insurrection based on the rebellion by Cataline, a sore loser who would not acknowledge his defeat in an election. There can be little doubt that Sallust's book provides an explanation that accords with similar rebellions in the present, such as in Brazil in 2023 and, before that, in the United States in 2021.

In short summary, Catiline, like Jair Bolsonaro in 2022 in Brazil, lost an election and refused to concede defeat. Instead of bowing out gracefully, he organized an insurrection, known to later generations as the Catiline conspiracy. What makes the Roman story so compelling—and relevant—in the light of the insurrection in Brasilia is that Catiline explicitly appealed to those "left behind" and claimed to side *with* the people against a corrupt elite. He promised simple solutions, like debt relief. Incidentally, Bolsonaro promised the same policy during the election in 2022.[81] Like the "Trump of the Tropics," as the defeated Brazilian politician was called,[82] Catiline promised that all would be resolved if the people followed him: "Use me as your commander," he exhorted. The parallels with history seem almost too uncanny to be spelled out. But Sallust is interesting not merely because he described a pattern that seems to repeat itself, but above all because he described the conditions that prevent democracies from falling apart and, more importantly, because he explained the mindset that leads to insurrections.

Why Men Rebel? This was the title of a study from the early 1970s in which Ted R. Gurr, in the non-gender neutral language of the time, sought to explain uprisings as a result of relative deprivation.[83] Gurr, a serious and judicious scholar, was adamant that "there is not much support for the view that political violence is primarily the recourse of vicious, criminal, deviant, ignorant, or undersocialized people." Rather, "discontented men [and women] are more susceptible to conversion to new beliefs than contented ones."[84] But Gurr was unable to explain the micro-foundations of this "conversion." Sometimes, he observed, that question was answered by pointing to precipitating events—elections and their results, protests that descend into anger, or the speeches of powerful demagogues. On other occasions, we blame insurrections on prejudices or bigotries—racism, xenophobia, anti-Semitism, and White nationalism, to name a few. This book does not seek to falsify Gurr. Rather, it seeks to provide neuropolitical explanations of patterns that he identified at the macrolevel. At the risk of being labeled a "positivist," this book seeks to return to the ideal (or dream) of unified science espoused by the likes of Otto Neurath and the logical positivists between the world wars.[85]

We should always draw on different perspectives. History provides one, psychology another, and social neuroscience yet another. The latter, by combining political science and biology, studies the phenomenon of rebellion, *not* from empathetic considerations of what it is like to be in the shoes of a revolutionary but rather from a perspective that looks at what happens in the brain when someone with the anger of a rebel is prompted to respond to external stimuli akin to those felt by insurrectionists. In other words, neuropolitics studies what happens neurophysiologically in our heads when we engage in revolutions and rebellions.

So, from a social neuroscience perspective, why do people take part in insurrections like the January 6, 2021, attack on the U.S. Capitol and the copycat attacks on the Brazilian Congress and Supreme Court on January 8, 2023? Why do they engage in political violence from a neuroscience point of view?[86] In line with the other chapters in this book, I suggest that we think about insurrections differently—because they originate in our brains. Indeed, I'd suggest that the insurrections in Washington, D.C., and Brasilia are due to overactivity in the amygdala—a primitive part of the brain that evolved millions of years ago, which we share with foxes and pigs.[87]

Social scientists used to focus on rational actions, as outlined in the introduction. But in recent years we have made great advances in understanding what goes on in the brain when we think politically. The biology of radical politics is no exception. Scholars have explored why people rebel for as long as there has been political science. In the early 1970s, one sociologist hypothesized that the reason was poverty, or "relative deprivation." Political scientists and economists, using sophisticated mathematical models, also tried to explain rebellion but found it hard to come up with a rational explanation. Very few people, the math showed, had any personal incentive to risk life and limb for the rather abstract benefits of overthrowing a government.

From a rational point of view, rebellions seem pointless. One political scientist even coined the phrase "the paradox of revolution." The same research—I have to admit—was the basis of papers that I published earlier in my career. In this research, I was at pains to show that the decision to engage in political violence was a rational one. But it turns out that rational choice, while sometimes accurate, only tells part of the story. So what are we to make of it all? Enter neuroscience. Since the early 2000s, when we, as the previous chapters have shown, have been able to look at what happens inside our heads when we think, we have also been able to understand what happens neurophysiologically when we rebel. Using functional magnetic resonance imaging (fMRI) scans, which measure changing blood flow to brain cells, we can now see which parts of the brain get activated when we engage in vari-ous activities, like shopping, thinking about sex, and feeling remorse.

As someone who, as previously mentioned, started out as a biologist before becoming a political scientist, what I personally found fascinating was how these two areas go so well together. Those two different academic fields offer a similar moral: To prevent revolutions we need to stay clear of a polarizing debate. This perspective has also entered the realm of political analysis—finally putting the "science" in political science. Of course, fMRI isn't useful for studying rebellions in real time; there's no way to scan people's brains at the moment they storm the palace. But we can design experiments that observe how people who share insurrectionist views react to hate speech and views that are articulated by politicians on the far right. By presenting subjects with statements about vulnerable minority groups during some brain scan studies, and showing them photos of political candidates they didn't agree with during others, researchers could literally see what was taking place in would-be insurrectionists' brains. Thus, when neurologist Giovanna Zamboni and colleagues conducted such an experiment a little over a decade ago, they found that a part of the brain known as the ventral striatum, which is associated with the limbic system, was activated when individuals who were identified by psychological tests as "radicals" were exposed to hate-speech statements or other intolerant assertions about other groups or minorities. These studies have been replicated in recent years and their findings confirmed and refined.

That the ventral striatum was activated is remarkable. This part of the brain is one of the oldest in evolutionary terms. It is what makes animals respond positively to simple rewards in social situations and megatively to stimuli in dangerous moments, such as fear that they might be attacked. The ventral striatum is linked to the amygdala, the fight-and-flight center in the brain. When people hear statements about—or see images of—groups or individuals that they fear, the brain reacts as if it is attacked. In contrast, study subjects who, based on personality tests, were identified as "moderate" or "conservative" used parts of the brain that only humans have evolved, such as the dorsolateral prefrontal cortex, which is responsible for planning and working memory and is associated with listening, speaking, and reasoning. In another study, from 2011, young people with far-right views showed greater activation of the amygdala, indicating that they were less likely to reflect on political statements and more likely to revert to fight-or-flight mode. The most interesting part of this body of research is that brains generally respond differently to politics than to policy. Scans show that when people think about *politics*—as in the rough and tumble partisan struggle—the fight-and-flight amygdala gets activated. But when people are exposed to questions about *policy*, they use the more advanced parts of the brain. In fMRI studies dating as far back as 2009, scientists found that the dorsolateral frontal cortex lit up in people exposed to arguments about economic policy.

Aristotle, way back in ancient Greece, believed that biology and politics go together. That is not a common view among scholars today. This view needs revision, for together these two different academic fields offer a similar lesson: To prevent rebellions and insurrections, we should avoid angry and polarized debate. And when possible, we should avoid political hot buttons and instead talk about the policy issues that affect our lives. In *The Republic* and in some of his earlier dialogues,[88] Plato talked about *thymos*—often translated as "spiritedness." This was not a negative thing entirely. There is a place for this feeling. Ideally, "the spirited part (in Greek, τὸ θυμοειδές) is the helper of reason by nature, unless it is corrupted by bad upbringing."[89]

Liya Yu, author of *Vulnerable Minds*, believes emotions are an important part of politics. They "drive us onto the streets, [make us] oppose dictators, and make us protest." Thus, "the picture that social neuro social and political neuroscience paints for us is a much more complex one in which what we hitherto saw as irrational emotions."[90] *Thymos* can be a wonderful thing if it is channeled towards higher things. In one of his earlier dialogues, Plato suggested that this spiritedness "glorifies the achievements of the past and ... teaches them to future generations."[91] But (and this was Plato's point) it can become destructive if citizens are animated by blind *thymos* and follow a demagogue out of spite and anger. In these situations, Plato, through Socrates, concluded that *thymos* would degenerate into a craze. The reason for this was that "madness can provide relief from the greatest plagues of trouble."[92] If you focus too much on that area, you are less likely to have defenses in place if you develop Alzheimer's disease. If we revert to these parts, we partially deprive ourselves of the advantages we have gained through eight million years of evolution. But neuropolitics also has something more positive to show us.

Chapter Three

Social Neuroscience, Political Attitudes, and Election Campaigns

In November 2015, the leader of Mexico's Institutional Revolutionary Party (PRI), Manlio Fabio Beltrones, said the party "would stick to tried and trusted campaign tools, like polls and political intuition," and rely on "the old-fashioned way" in its future campaigns, reported the *New York Times*.[93] A story like this would usually seem rather mundane and unimportant, but from our perspective, it was not. Indeed, the vow to stick to the tried and tested came after the prominent American newspaper had reported (or revealed) that the then-governing Mexican party had used neuropolitical techniques to win votes. The newspaper had discovered that "President Enrique Peña Nieto's campaign and his party, the Institutional Revolutionary Party, or PRI, employed tools to measure voters' brain waves, skin arousal, heart rates, and facial expressions during the 2012 presidential campaign."

In light of what we have seen in previous chapters, the PRI had not been particularly sophisticated. They had merely utilized research that neuropolitics pioneers had developed a decade before. The scientists' research had focused on the amygdala, the by now familiar and evolutionarily very old part of the brain, which the reader by now will know is, *inter alia,* associated with fear and fight responses. What the researchers had found using fMRI scans was that "the human amygdala processes both the degree of emotion in facial expressions and the categorical ambiguity of the emotion shown."[94] This little piece of information was rather creatively picked up by the PRI. They wanted to know if the impressions of their candidates would prompt different facial expressions, which—albeit indirectly—could help them gauge the voters' propensity to vote PRI. The theory was that if you like something, the amygdala responds in a particular way, and this is shown in the facial expression. The Mexican party officials and their advisors found this very useful, especially in trying to find out how well a campaign slogan worked.

So, what did the Mexicans do in practice? At the entrance to several buildings there was a photo of the candidate, but there was a secret camera behind it, which recorded these by passers' expressions, and *presto*, PRI could determine if the candidate inspired trust—or not! Not brain scans, to be sure, but research based on findings from neuropolitics, nonetheless. The PRI promised to mend their ways. This is the usual pattern. Political campaigns and parties have always been reluctant to admit to using such dark arts. But the protestations of the PRI notwithstanding, the techniques have not gone away from Mexican political campaigning. In any case, it is certainly interesting that Vladimir Humberto Herrera Aquino, a Mexican political consultant, wrote an article a few years later which, in English translation, had the title "Neuropolitics, a new way to win elections."'[95] So, maybe we are already living in the world of neuropolitics without knowing it?

There is no point in speculating. This book is not a piece of investigative journalism but one of popular political science.

So, let's take a step back and look at the brain science of political behavior and where we are up to now. To make sense of all this, it might be good to have an overview of where we are as regards the various centers of the brain that are associated with political thinking. In an early book that touched upon this issue, political psychologist Drew Westen pointed out that:

> Roughly speaking, two broad regions of the prefrontal cortex are worth discussing [from a political point of view]. Toward the top and sides of the frontal lobes is the dorsolateral prefrontal cortex.... This part of the brain is always active when people are making conscious choices....The other region of the prefrontal cortex, peering out from behind the eyes and extending about halfway up the forehead, is the ventromedial prefrontal cortex.... [It is] involved in social and emotional experience, social and emotional intelligence, and moral functioning. It also plays a crucial role in linking thought and emotion, particularly in using emotional reactions to guide decision making. Not surprisingly, this region has dense neural connections with cerebral structures below the cortex involved in generation emotional states, such as the amygdala.[96]

Mr. Westen, who was explicitly and openly liberal, found it "tempting to map our current political topography onto these two regions of the prefrontal cortex."[97] He suggested that Democrats were more likely to draw on the dorsolateral prefrontal cortex, whereas Republicans were more emotional and were guided more by excitement and gut feelings than by rational reasoning. Today, we know this is an oversimplification. Indeed, there are indications that the dorsolateral prefrontal cortex lights up in the brains of conservatives as well, as this part of the brain is also associated with inhibition and caution—traits that are associated with being on the right of the political spectrum. That Mr. Westen got it slightly wrong is not an indictment. It is part of good scientific practice. As good researchers, we know we make scientific progress not through verification but by learning from our mistakes and by proposing falsifiable hypotheses, which we gradually falsify to get a more accurate picture of reality.[98]

So, given that neuroscience moves on and learns from mistakes like any other proper science, what is the state of our knowledge today? What are the theories yet to be falsified? And how do they pertain to neuropolitics? In the previous chapter, we encountered John Jost's motivated social cognition model. It essentially says that holding conservative views is a way of coping with threats. Thus, "chronically and temporarily activated needs to reduce uncertainty, ambiguity, threat, and disgust ... are positively associated with conservatism."[99] You probably don't need a degree in sociology to come up with that. Indeed, there are any number of perceptive and impressive ethnographic studies that reach this conclusion based on participant observation and qualitative studies, such as Hochschild's sociological study *Strangers in Their Own Land*.[100]

One of the conclusions in these studies of Trump supporters and those who voted for Brexit in the UK was that they perceived themselves to be under threat. What we are interested in from a neuropolitical point of view is how this manifests itself in the brain. Not, mind you, because we believe in some kind of reductionism, but because this perspective complements the more traditional social science and humanities perspective. So, what do we know? Certainly, other scholars have come to some of the same conclusions. Whether conservative or not, it is a consistent finding that "emotion, decision making and the orbitofrontal cortex" are associated when people make political choices.[101]

But can this research make a difference? And how does it compare to traditional political science? Well, for starters, neuropolitics has presented some rather remarkable findings. For example, that we can predict individuals' political ideology with 85 percent accuracy.[102] Compare this to the more traditional methods that base such predictions on the parents' political leanings, which can only predict ideology with 65 percent accuracy,[103] and you ought to be impressed. Yet, some are unconvinced and have said that these researchers are "overstating the definitiveness of its theoretical implications."[104] That might always be the case, especially if we are basing these conclusions on a small number of studies, but when the same results point in the same direction when the initial findings are being corroborated, these criticisms then become more difficult to sustain. And studies have shown that we *can* draw theoretical and politically relevant implications from these findings.

Using so-called "multidimensional scaling and parametric functional magnetic resonance imaging to identify which criteria/dimensions people use to structure complex political beliefs and which brain regions are concurrently activated," Zambioni and colleagues found that

three independent dimensions explained the variability of
a set of statements expressing political beliefs and that each
dimension was reflected in a distinctive pattern of neural
activation: individualism (medial prefrontal cortex and temporoparietal junction), conservatism (dorsolateral prefrontal
cortex), and radicalism (ventral striatum and posterior cingulate). The structures we identified are also known to be important in self–other processing, social decision-making in
ambivalent situations, and reward prediction. Our results ex-
tend current knowledge on the neural correlates of the structure of political beliefs, a fundamental aspect of the human
ability to coalesce into social entities.[105]

This might require a bit of explanation, as these regions might
not be familiar to the reader. What this study basically shows
is that those who are conservatives activate the dorsolateral
prefrontal cortex, which is associated with caution—in line
with the findings by Jost (see above). Conservatives, as the
term implies, are guarded and want things to stay the same.
So, it stands to reason that they activate a part of the brain
that is also associated with aversion to risk-taking.[106] What is
also interesting is that radicals—those who are more likely to
support populist policies—are driven more by the activation
of more evolutionarily primitive parts of the brain and are
more likely to go for what we might call instant gratification.
The reported findings that the ventral striatum is activated
among those associated with radicalism are interesting. This
part of the so-called basal ganglia (a structure under the surface) is widely reported to be involved in "social comparison
on reward processing in the human brain."[107]

But the evidence, in fairness, is not totally conclusive, and
there are subtle differences. Other studies have found slight

differences. A study that received considerable press—at least within neuropolitics circles—was "Political Orientations Are Correlated with Brain Structure in Young Adults." The reason why this paper got more than its fair share of attention was because one of the co-authors was the British actor Colin Firth—the man who played Mr. Darcy in *Bridget Jones's Diary* and starred in the BBC's adaptation of *Pride and Prejudice*.

In the study, the researchers found that "substantial differences exist in the cognitive styles of liberals and conservatives on psychological measures." Thus, in a sample of young adults, the researchers "related self-reported political attitudes to gray matter volume using structural MRI" and found that "greater liberalism was associated with increased gray matter volume in the anterior cingulate cortex."[108] This, again, needs to be explained. The anterior cingulate cortex is a part of that brain that lies at the front part of the central sulcus, the valley that separates the two brain hemispheres. This part of the cerebrum has been shown in other studies to be associated with empathy,[109] which might be consistent with the tendency of liberal and more socialist voters to have a greater sense of social justice and concern for the least well-off.[110]

But Firth and colleagues also found something that may be similar to what we saw in the previous chapter on populism. Thus, they found that "greater conservatism was associated with increased volume of the right amygdala,"[111] a part of the brain that is—as we have seen—associated with more visceral responses. That these findings were subsequently "replicated in an independent sample of additional participants," needless to say, make them more trustworthy.

Yet, as good researchers, Firth and colleagues acknowledged that we have to be cautious, and they duly admitted that their "data do not determine whether these regions play a causal role in the formation of political attitudes." Nevertheless, they also argue that their findings "converge with previous work to suggest a possible link between brain structure and psychological mechanisms that mediate political attitudes." By linking their findings to earlier studies indicating something along the same lines, they clearly corroborated their findings. Thus, their work showed something that had been found in cross-cultural studies—as they pointed out in the article.

One of the arguments against traditional social science and philosophy is that they are biased and reflect Western norms and cultures. Political science, as a social science that developed to analyze voters and politicians in American and European societies, may not be good at understanding and analyzing individuals who do not live in these societies. The same criticism could be leveled at neuropolitics, except that some of the findings suggest that these patterns have cross-cultural validity. This, certainly, was the conclusion of a study that compared American and Japanese voters. Nicholas O. Rule and colleagues found that candidates for whom participants from both countries chose to vote "elicited stronger responses in the bilateral amygdala than candidates for whom participants chose not to vote" and that this finding was "true regardless of either the participant's culture or the target's culture," which suggested that "these voting decisions provoked the same neural response cross-culturally."[112]

So, when Darren Schreiber and colleagues were able to observe differences between "red" and "blue" brains, they were not just reporting on an American phenomenon. The same pattern is seen in other places too, even if more research is needed to draw firmer conclusions.[113]

So, in terms of identifying patterns, neuropolitics arguably has an edge in being able to provide findings that transcend cultural differences—albeit within developed capitalist societies. But can we trust these findings more generally? And isn't it a problem that all these studies were based on self-reported political identification? Well, there is a way of overcoming this. Psychologists have developed a so-called *Implicit Association Test* to disclose what we really think about race, gender stereotypes and so on.[114]

In a study that is often cited in the emerging literature on neuropolitics, Knutson and colleagues "assessed political attitudes using the Implicit Association Test (IAT) in which participants were presented faces and names of well-known Democrat and Republican politicians along with positive and negative words while undergoing functional MRI." They "found a significant behavioral IAT effect for the face, but not the name, condition."[115] In particular, they found that "amygdala and fusiform gyrus were activated during perceptual processing of familiar faces." The fusiform gyrus is a large area in the lower part of the temporal cortex, which plays important roles in object and face recognition, so this is not, in itself, surprising.[116]

But what was more interesting from a political science point of view was that "frontopolar activation was positively correlated with an implicit measure of bias ... (how strongly the participants felt about the politicians), while strength of affiliation with political party was negatively correlated with lateral PFC [prefrontal cortex]," which, in their view, gave credence to the "idea that two distinct but interacting networks—one emphasizing rapid, stereotypic, and emotional associative knowledge and the other emphasizing more deliberative and factual knowledge—co-operate in the processing of politicians."[117] Thus, when evaluating politicians, we are driven by gut feelings but also, occasionally, if we like them, by more reasoned thinking.

In Knutson and colleagues' summary, their "findings of ventromedial PFC activation suggests that when processing the associative knowledge concerned with politicians, stereotypic knowledge is activated, but in addition, the anterior prefrontal activations indicate that more elaborative, reflective knowledge about the politician is activated."[118]

Now, this is all well, but it rather risks stating the bleedingly obvious. To say that we are sometimes biased and sometimes base our decisions on deliberation is not really that path-breaking. What we need to show is when we do the former rather than the latter. So, an obvious question would be, when are we biased? When is it that, say, a photo of a politician elicits an emotional response that can be detected by an activated amygdala in an fMRI scan?

This is exactly the question Michael Spezio and colleagues set out to investigate in "A Neural Basis for the Effect of Candidate Appearance on Election Outcomes." What they found was that "election outcomes correlate with judgments based on a candidate's visual appearance, suggesting that the attributions viewers make based on appearance, so-called thin-slice judgments, influence voting."[119] But they also found that "images of losing candidates elicited greater activation in the insula and ventral anterior cingulate."[120] Why exactly this is so is less obvious. The insula is an area associated with empathy, whereas the ventral anterior cingulate cortex is associated with social evaluation.[121] So, maybe this piece of research suggests that we feel sorry for losers. In this age of hate speech, this could be a nice touch, but it is not something we can conclusively prove.

Does all this give us a positive view of politics? Is it good to be politically involved? Most of us would think so.

The problem with a passion for politics

Not long after leaving university, I had a job in the British Home Office, the UK ministry that was responsible for elections. The minister was David Blunkett, a robust and impressive Yorkshireman who had overcome Dickensian poverty and blindness to become one of the most influential men in the country. For him it was politics and political engagement that had taken him from poverty in Sheffield to power in SW1.[122] As I recall him saying, "interest in politics is always a good thing. We must do everything we can to get people involved in politics, get them to vote. That is the start of any civilized and democratic society."[123]

It is difficult to disagree with this sentiment. But the findings of neuropolitics somewhat qualify the panacea-like fervor of Mr. Blunkett. In fact, some of the findings rather suggest that too much political interest might not be so great after all. This, at any rate, is what Marta Gozzi and colleagues found in their paper titled "Interest in Politics Modulates Neural Activity in the Amygdala and Ventral Striatum."[124] They "scanned individuals (either interested or uninterested in politics based on a self-report questionnaire) while they were expressing their agreement or disagreement with political opinions." After the scanning, "participants were asked to rate each political opinion presented in the scanner for emotional valence and emotional intensity." What they found was, rather alarmingly (if you share Blunkett's view), that "individuals interested in politics showed greater activation in the amygdala and the ventral striatum (ventral putamen) relative to individuals uninterested in politics when reading political opinions in accordance with their own views."[125] And they concluded that "this study shows that having an interest in politics elicits activations in emotion- and reward-related brain areas even when simply agreeing with written political opinions.[126]

By this stage, the reader should be able to draw conclusions from this study, at least as far as the amygdala is concerned. As we have seen in the previous chapter and in the above-mentioned study by Firth and colleagues, the amygdala is activated when people are angry and fearful and constitutes a part of the brain that is—from an evolutionary perspective—rather primitive. So, to put it crudely, those who are interested in politics are not necessarily the most cerebral; they rely on gut feelings and not necessarily on deliberation.

But the study also found that the ventral striatum (in particular the ventral putamen) is activated. What does this

mean? And what is this part of the brain known for? The ventral putamen (ventral is Latin for "belly side") is part of the
basal ganglia, which we have already encountered. It is, put
rather crudely again, a part of the reward system. That is not a
problem, of course; rewards are an important part of a healthy
psychological process. Indeed, the putamen is involved in
learning and motor control, including speech articulation,
language functions, reward, and cognitive functioning.[127] But
it is also involved in addiction and is associated with some less
attractive traits, such as obsessive gambling.[128] The putamen,
combined with the globus pallidus, forms the lentiform nucleus; and with the caudate nucleus, it shapes the striatum,
which is a subcortical structure that forms the basal ganglia.

So, the fact—if we are to believe Gozzi and colleagues—
that those interested in politics really show greater activation
of the centers of the brain associated with addiction and ag-
gression is not a great advertisement for political engagement.
As it happens, this is not a new or exceptional finding. In the
1960s, political sociologists Almond and Verba suggested
that political systems work best if people are not constantly
engaged in politics. They espoused, based on interviews with
voters, a so-called *civic culture* in which citizens did not deplete
their "civic reserves" but kept them in store for when things
went wrong.[129] In a way, this finding chimes with—and is supported by—the recent findings of neuropolitics.

So, can all this knowledge be used in practical politics?
Say, to win elections. Perhaps that is the wrong question? Perhaps these techniques have already been used? Certainly, the
example from Mexico cited at the beginning of this chapter
seems to indicate this. We will turn to this now.

Elections and neuromarketing

"It is certain," said an article in *Forbes Magazine*, "that campaigns are using or plan to use neuromarketing as a tool to understand voter reactions and preferences, as well as evaluate campaign ads."[130] Some might be shocked to hear this. After all, we don't like the idea that our democratic decisions are influenced by political consultants and spin doctors who manipulate our minds and make us vote for causes we do not support. And yet, we may be deceiving ourselves if we entertain the thought that politics is a clean game where we are merely deciding whom to vote for after careful deliberation and weighing up preferences. Certainly, there is an element of this (and the neuropolitical reasons for that are a subject to which we shall return in the next chapter). But it cannot be denied that electoral politics is shaped by paid professionals.

In fact, a case could be made for the view that political consultants have existed as long as democracy itself. For example, the *sophists* made infamous by Plato were arguably nothing more than the political consultants of fifth-century BCE Athens. Indeed, in his dialogue *Protagoras*, Plato explicitly defined a sophist as someone who teaches "how to realize one's maximum potential for success in political debate and action."[131] Plato's pupil Aristotle even wrote a whole treatise on the subject. Other writers in this tradition include the Roman politician and philosopher Marcus Cicero, who wrote eloquently on the art of persuasion. And, in a more practical vein, his brother Quintus Cicero wrote *Commentariolum petitionis*, a detailed handbook for his brother's consular election campaign, complete with dirty tricks and cunning tactics based on rhetoric.[132]

In the twentieth century, these tactics were finessed by the use of target polls, focus groups, and the like. And to add to this, in recent years, political consultants have used AI and online targeting to find voters. For example, in the 2016 Brexit campaign, Victoria Woodcock—the operations director of *Vote Leave*—developed a new "canvasing software," which effectively identified voters who would potentially vote leave. Utilizing this, the Brexiteer campaigners then asked members of the public to enter a competition where they could win £50 million if they could correctly identify the correct result of each of the fifty-one matches in the Euro 2016 football tournament. The only "price" for entering was to give Vote Leave their mobile number and email address and to answer how much on a scale from 1–10 the respondent hated the EU. Millions signed up. Drawing on this information, they signed up the Canadian-based company *AggregateIQ* to channel money to social media companies,[133] "including $1.7m to Facebook for 146m paid impressions. In total, Vote Leave delivered 309m online ads during the ten weeks [of official campaigning] and an impressive 890m Facebook impressions between October 2015 and 23 June 2016."[134]

This is not to get carried away with writing about the dark arts of campaigning but merely to set the scene for the next chapter in the story—the emergence of neuromarketing. The big question is whether the use of these techniques is realistic. As we have seen in the introduction, the answer to that question is in the affirmative, as the case of the PRI campaign in

Mexico showed. But to what degree and how? The most fundamental question is what can neuromarketing do? How does it work, and how does it relate to general neuropolitics?

At the most fundamental level, neuromarketing utilizes our knowledge of certain parts of the brain involved in inhibition (it's that dorsolateral prefrontal cortex again) but also other parts such as the insula which shows empathy. But, as is always the case with neuroscience, the lessons are drawn from a controlled experiment, which we subsequently try to extrapolate to a wider population.

Political consultants—for reasons outlined above—have been reluctant to share their insights. So, before we try to discern them, let's start with an example from product advertising. Chocolate is a popular product. But are we likely to shift from Mars bars to Ritter? Or from Lindor to Cadbury?

Which is a better predictor of purchasing behavior—qualitative research or fMRI scans? In a study, three German researchers subjected eighteen chocoholics (all women between the ages of 23 and 56) to a simple experiment.[135] The women were shown a photo of a Duplo Bar (one of the best-selling German chocolate products) and six other products (including a toothbrush) for two seconds, followed by a three-second display of an ad for Duplo, then the product again for two seconds. After this, the women were asked to rank the products according to their preference. The researchers were able to create three sales forecasts: one based on each of the women's stated preference, another based on brain activity during viewing of the ads, and finally, one based on fMRI changes to product viewing before and after communications. The authors reported that "the fMRI imaging of participants during marketing communications (B) predicted sales (D) better than subjects' stated preference (A)."[136]

Their other conclusion—which we need to clarify later was—"that ROIs consisting of NAcc, mOFC, Amyg, HC, IFG, dmPFC ... were assumed to contribute positively to later sales and DLPFC and Ins ... were predicted to contribute negatively to sales."[137] Again, this is rather forbidding language, so let's break it down. In fact, it is not quite as difficult to understand as it seems. We need not focus on all the acronyms but only the ones the authors singled out as most important. The main ones the researchers drew attention to were NAcc and DLPFC, respectively. The latter—the dorsolateral pre-frontal cortex—we have already met; it is the part of the brain associated with inhibition, the one that we often see in people who are of a conservative persuasion. The former stands for the *nucleus accumbens*—a part of the midbrain deep below the surface of the frontal lobes. Now, what is interesting is that this part of the brain has been shown to be associated with the Pavlovian reflexes known from psychology.[138] (The reader will recall that Pavlov's dog salivated when it associated the sound of a bell with food.) If we add to this that the nucleus accumbens (henceforth, NAcc) is also associated with desire and motivation, it is probably not surprising that these parts of the brain were activated in those of the women who craved chocolate. Nor is it surprising that the dorsolateral prefrontal cortex inhibited these responses in others. So, what are we to make of this? Basically this: that advertisements can create a Pavlovian reflex that make us (artificially) crave chocolate.

The big question then is whether a similar mechanism could be in play for political "tastes." To answer this question, we need to look closer at the NAcc which is part of the *striatum* (also known as the striate nucleus), a cluster of neurons in the so-called basal ganglia in the forebrain. The striatum is an important component of what is known as the motor and reward systems.

Overall, then, can we see differences in different political persuasions? There are indications that we can. This has been succinctly put in a research paper:

> Liberals have been found to exhibit increased brain activity and more grey matter volume in the anterior cingulate cortex, a brain region important for detecting cognitive conflict. Furthermore, conservatives have been found to possess more grey matter volume in the amygdala, a region that detects motivationally salient objects, including threatening stimuli. These studies have helped to establish a growing body of research linking political beliefs and personality traits to specific neuropsychological and psychophysiological substrates.[139]

One of the findings of political science more generally is that negative advertising has an effect on party preferences. What is new is that this can be seen in brain scans as well. We, once again, turn to the *dorsolateral prefrontal cortex* (DLPFC). This part of the brain is involved in decision-making,[140] which is why it has been of particular interest to economists using brain scans.[141]

Now, what is interesting in a political context is that "heightened DLPFC activity has been observed in those who change their candidate preferences in response to negative political advertising."[142] How exactly did this insight come about? The authors carried out a simple experiment. Eight women and 32 men were

> presented videos from previous electoral campaigns and tele-
> vision commercials for major cola brands and then used the
> subjects' self-rated affinity toward political candidates as be-
> havioural indicators. After viewing negative campaign videos,
> subjects showing stronger fMRI activation in the dorsolateral
> prefrontal cortex lowered their ratings of the candidate they
> originally supported more than did those with smaller fMRI
> signal changes in the same region."[143]

But what was perhaps more interesting—at least from a political science perspective—was that the same negative effect
could not be observed when the subjects were shown negative
ads about brands of cola.

Figure 1 shows that the signal change was negatively correlated with the previous preference for the politician. In other
words, the more exposure to the ad, the lower the signal.
Admittedly, the Pearson coefficient is relatively low, at R=.33
(significant at p>0.05), which is a medium correlation. Still,
it shows something about neuropolitics that few were aware
of, and, in any case, this correlation is as good as what we get
in most sociological studies of political behavior. If you look
at the bar chart, this gives an even clearer impression of the
differences between politics and beverages. As you can see,
there is a massive change in the three columns representing
negative ads about politicians—not so for the columns on the
right, that is, those representing two different cola brands.

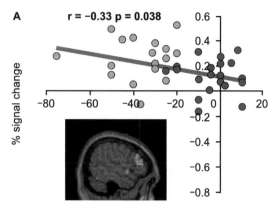

Preference Change for Attacked Candidate

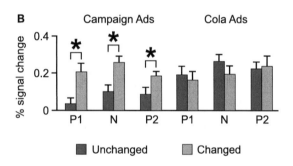

Figure 1: Signal Change and Preference for Candidate[144]

So, the neuropolitical findings show a distinct effect for political ads—something, we might add, that has been rather difficult to show using the conventional tools of political analysis.[145] What this research does, then, is not to render conventional political science and sociology methods redundant but rather adds another dimension to the process of mixed-methods triangulation that is essential in all path-breaking research.

Admittedly, the research is still in its infancy, and there are still many things we do not know about the brain. This is especially true in regards to how stimuli both affect and effect physiological processes that go on in the brain. However, the fact that we are able to detect when people are on the right and on the left and to identify areas and regions of the cortex that, through functional connectivity, reveal underlying preferences is a giant step forward for political science and analysis.

Chapter Four

The Listening Brain: The State We Ought to Be In

"We are not what we know but what we are willing to learn."[146] Mary Catherine Bateson (1939–2021), the cultural anthropologist, always used this motto to convey her tolerance and openness to other cultures and her conviction that the essence of humanity is a willingness to listen. The daughter of the ethnographer power couple Margaret Mead and Gregory Bateson, she grew up in an enlightened New York household where openness to other voices, preferably in their native tongues, was the order of the day. Mary herself was a polyglot and spoke at least ten foreign languages. Pithy though it was, her strapline was not unique. Others, too, have expressed the same sentiment—and the same philosophy of life. The Dalai Lama, to name but one, has remarked: "When you talk, you are only repeating what you already know. But if you listen, you may learn something new."

Nothing, it seems, could be further from the adversarial and occasionally cutthroat attitude that characterizes politics today. The openness and acceptance of others that lie at the heart of these quotes seem to be the polar opposite—the antithesis, if you like—of the political debates we encounter on Twitter and other not always "social" media.

The controversial social and legal theorist Carl Schmitt (1888–1985) remarked that "we contrast good and bad in ethics, beautiful and ugly in aesthetics," but that the "specific juxtaposition to which all political actions and attitudes can be reduced is that between friend and enemy."[147] In the light of such definitions, it is tempting to conclude that openness and tolerance, and ultimately respect for other people, are incompatible with politics; that this is just an adversarial game of us versus them.

But there is reason to be cautious and not get carried away. Certainly, the shorthand of friend versus enemy is neat and diabolically elegant, but that does not make it right. Schmitt openly supported dictatorship and even joined the ranks of the tyrants after 1933.

Perhaps today Schmitt's juxtaposition contains a kernel of truth even in democracies. But we should not be bowled over backwards by neat definitions. Eloquence does not establish a fact. The friend-enemy dichotomy was conceived in the dying days of the Weimar Republic, at a time when enmity was the order of the day and where angry mobs clashed in the streets. That this definition chimes with what we are witnessing today is a cause for concern. It is a worrying indication of just how far we have drifted from the ideals of democratic governance espoused by those who defended what Abraham Lincoln famously described as "government of the people, by the people, for the people."[148]

Certainly, there are camps, parties, and what used to be called "fractions"[149] in places where the voters are the ultimate masters. But politics in democracies is so much more than adversarial. We know this in our heart of hearts. Yes, cynics may contend that those who speak of "the common good" are romantic and possibly even naïve. This objection, rather conveniently, overlooks that many democratic societies have written this common goal in their names—the Commonwealth of Virginia, for example, and the Commonwealth of Australia. In these cases, it is explicit that we are not enemies, but in it together. That this is so is not just a quirk of English-speaking countries. The Swedish word for society, *samhället*, literally translates as "that which holds us together." And *samfund*, the Danish word for the same, is etymologically "that which we have discovered together."

The ancient Greeks also had a word for it, one that illustrated this element of being in it together, but also that of discovering something in unison, of learning from one another. This is the one we find in the ancient treaties and in the descriptions of how they conducted public affairs. The word was *bouleúō*—"to take counsel." Their legislative assembly—the *boule* (from the same word)—was literally the place where 500 randomly selected citizens would make decisions after they had listened and taken counsel, not where they fought as friends and enemies. Democratic politics in ancient Greece was the art of listening to advice and learning from others—the art of *bouleusis*. The aim was not to win the argument but to solve problems; it was not about ultimate "ends but about means," about considering—through *bouleúō*—"how and by what means good government can be achieved."[150]

Whereas political discussions in modern times—and at times of upheaval more generally—are characterized by point-scoring and being right, in this day and age, we are obsessed with winning the argument. Just think of the public debates between candidates before elections. Rather than focusing on the substance, we are preoccupied with polls showing who landed the best blows and who "won."

The Athenians' democracy was not all perfect; they too had so-called *sophists* who sought to persuade voters with lofty rhetoric (see the previous chapter). But the tenor of the democratic system of the Greeks was one that was based on reasoning, or *nous*, as it was called. Even such a critic of Athenian democracy as the historian Thucydides wrote that Athenian democracy was permeated by "a spirit of reverence [for] public acts." And, in contrast to the hyperpartisanship of many present-day democracies, the Athenians were "prevented from doing wrong by respect for the authorities and for the laws."[151] The reason for this was not just due to the institutions but also a consequence of their attitude toward politics. Hence, the ideal of *bouleúō* was to "take others into our deliberations, distrusting our own capacity to decide" on the matter.[152]

It is easy to eulogize the Athenians and elevate their political system to Olympian heights. It is important not to do so. And we should never forget that theirs was also a sexist society, where only men could vote, and, moreover, one based on slave ownership. Moreover, it was a system that was responsible for executing Socrates in what amounts to perhaps the most infamous miscarriage of justice in history. The Athenians were not angels. "The weak suffer what they must" was their attitude toward a small country that refused to bow to their naval superiority.[153] But for all their documented flaws, the Athenians—and more so than any of the other democracies of the ancient world—provided an ideal that has been the basis for subsequent imperfect democracies ever since.

In the wake of the English Civil War in the 1640s, the philosopher Thomas Hobbes (1588–1679) believed that a *Leviathan*—"a mortal god"—was necessary to keep the peace.[154] Yet, places ruled by one man—as this philosopher espoused—have not kept the peace. Anything but, in fact. They have been violent places and have had poor relations with their neighbors: "All international wars since World War I have involved dictatorships. Two-thirds of civil wars and ethnic conflicts since World War II have erupted in countries under authoritarian rule."[155] Countries ruled by an unelected and unaccountable few have also tended to be poorer. Twenty-three of the top 25 countries on the United Nations Development Program's (UNDP) list of the most prosperous countries are democracies.[156]

Why is this so? Once again, the ancient Greeks had an answer. The philosopher Aristotle (384–322 BCE) was the teacher to Alexander the Great. But being the tutor for a man who effectively became the ruler of the whole known world did not mean that Aristotle eulogized rule by a single individual. He was clear that it was far better to allow citizens to reach decisions through listening, talking, and learning from each other through careful deliberation. He was not preachy, but matter-of-factual when he reported that democracies worked because they allowed citizens to combine their knowledge, "for although each individual separately will be a worse judge than the experts, the whole of them [the people] assembled together will be better judges." He went on:

> It is possible that the many, though not individually good men, yet when they come together may be better, not individually but collectively, than those who are so, just as public dinners to which many contribute are better than those supplied at one man's cost; for where there are many, each individual, it may be argued, has some portion of virtue and wisdom, and when they have come together, just as the multitude becomes a single man with many feet and many hands and many senses, so also it becomes one personality as regards the moral and intellectual faculties.[157]

Clearly then, it was all to do with listening and learning.

Aristotle, unquestionably, the greatest scientist of the ancient world, was an open-minded chap, and as the founder of the discipline of zoology, it is probably not surprising that he briefly pondered whether the same "wisdom of the crowds"— as it has been called—"would also apply to animals."[158] Unable to answer the question, he swiftly moved on.

So, why do we have this ability to listen, to learn, and to deliberate? The answer was found in an article written by zoologists who published an article in a scientific journal 2300 years after Aristotle had left the question unanswered.

"Human speech and language," they wrote, "are communication abilities that are without parallel in the animal kingdom."[159] A definitive and bold statement, and yet one written as if the authors were blissfully unaware of the immense implications of this simple fact. For this apparent throw-away remark, in a sense, is the key to understanding *all* civilizations and the full span of human history. Perhaps unwittingly, the authors of the biological article expressed something that fundamentally explains why *homo sapiens* is the species that built the pyramids and dug the Panama Canal, and that it took a human brain to produce the music of Charlie Parker and modern jazz.

This almost off-the-cuff remark lends scientific credence to the uniqueness of humans, but others have been on to the same idea. "There are no men," wrote the philosopher René Descartes (1596–1650), "not even the insane, so dull and stupid that they cannot put words together in a manner to convey their thoughts. On the contrary, there is no other animal however perfect and fortunately situated it may be, that can do the same."[160] Presumably, the sexist language does not exclude women. In any case, the gist is the same. Humans can speak and listen; other species cannot. While there are studies that show that bonobos (a closer relative to humans than even the common chimp) can learn simple sign language commands,[161] no other primate can teach or learn from each other through language. None!

So, why are we so unique? Can't other primates make sounds? Not in the way that we can. To be sure, chimpanzees can make vocal noises, some of which show that our near-nearest relatives in the animal kingdom have a kind of language,[162] but at best, other primates can merely point to things or express displeasure. This may all be very interesting to the zoologist, and even impressive to the lay person, but ultimately it is nothing that begins to compare with humans.

This is where neuropolitics once more enters the fray. A simple fMRI scan of the human brain reveals that we have exceptionally developed areas for speech and listening, and moreover, that we can learn by exchanging views in a free and open discussion.

We have already looked at the amygdala, and the reader could be excused for thinking that we are but primitive beings that are visceral and angry. But, of course, our brains are more than that.

Look at an fMRI scan of the brain when it is exposed to a simple political argument on economic policy. Now the part that lights up (striped area in Fig. 2), this time in the dorsolateral frontal cortex, is the part associated not only with listening, speaking, and reasoning but also with caution. A person might sometimes be driven by amygdala responses. But this same person can also make rational arguments. We humans all have the capacity to use the powers with which we have been endowed by evolution. When we do so, we not only solve problems in society but also engage our brains, which, as research shows, makes us less likely to develop degenerative conditions like Alzheimer's and Parkinson's.

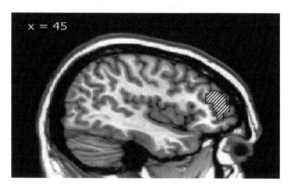

Figure 2: fMRI Scan of the DLPFC[163]

But, if we choose a different path, we begin our descent down the evolutionary ladder. We have a choice to make.

The evolution of the speech centers gave homo sapiens the brain power to cooperate and, combined with the vocal cords, the capacity to exchange views and learn from each other. In a sense, the rest is history—the history that we are about to tell, the story of the listening brain, the one capable of engaging in *bouleusis*.

The most important part of the first chapter of our evolution of the democratic brain is the ability to engage in conversation. This ability stems from the give and take of communication. This capacity is due to two specific areas of the brain. These are called, respectively, the *Broca area* (associated with speech) and the *Wernicke area* (associated with listening).

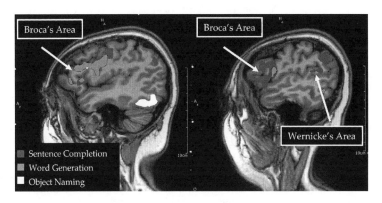

Figure 3: fMRI Scan of the Broca and Wernicke Areas[164]

The figure above shows areas activated during discussion, namely sentence completion, word generation, and object naming. As the fMRI scan shows, we activate many different parts of the brain when we discuss policy, the Wernicke and Broca areas, but also the dorsolateral prefrontal cortex, which is associated with decision making. Discussion is listening and talking before making up our minds.

Uniquely among species, we have this ability to make decisions after we have listened. And we can, in turn, prompt others to make choices. We thus, have a listening—or, if you like, a democratic—brain. For, discussion is a two-way street; it is talking as much as listening. "At the heart of a strong democracy is talk," wrote the American writer and scholar Benjamin Barber.[165] And it is this democratic brain in action we see on the scan.

The essence of this briefest of summaries of the language centers in our brains shows what happens when we engage in discussion. We do not, for rather obvious reasons, have brain scans of the Athenian males who were gathered to "take counsel" in the *boule*—the legislative assembly—over two thousand years ago. But if we did, it is a fair bet that we would get images akin to the ones shown above.

Why is all of this so important? Mainly because other species do not have this capacity. To be sure, we still have parts of the brain that we share with other animals. We, too, have the fight-and-flight part that allows us to react with vigor and rage when this is necessary—and occasionally when it isn't.

What is important is that our whole evolution as an *animal socialis*—a social being—hinges on the unique ability to communicate through language.[166] What scans show and what our knowledge of neuroscience teaches us is that we have been successful because we have these capabilities—this knack for learning through listening. If we do not use this ability, if we simply act by instinct, we are certainly not fulfilling our evolutionary potential. And who knows, perhaps we might even go backwards on the evolutionary ladder.

We are not merely created for rage and impulse, nor for compassion and sympathy; rather, we are able to use our capacity for communication to improve our condition and to learn through it. Of course, this ability would be of little use if we did not have other higher faculties too. Solving problems together, that is, "taking counsel," is useful only because we can put the knowledge to good use through all the other capabilities we have thanks to other parts of the brain.

But it is listening that is of the most crucial importance here. We have a democratic brain because this form of government at its heart is based on *bouleúō*, or, as we may translate it here, "deliberative listening." We have the capacity to listen and learn. We are not like animals, like birds and bees. Our decisions are, or ought to be, made after we have weighed up the facts, the pros and cons—in short, after a discussion. That we have evolved societies, that we have moved beyond just living a hand-to-mouth existence on the savannah, is because we have utilized this listening brain. But to continue to do so, we need to exercise caution lest we fall backwards into anger and react instinctively rather than through reflection. We need to utilize and exercise the higher cortex that brought us here and not to always fall back on a limbic system that is designed to be used only in case of emergency. And to do so means, above all, to engage in *bouleusis*.

Democracy—in the way it was described by the Greek authors—was rather practical. It was an exercise in problem-solving. The aim was not merely to win support for our ideas and get others to vote for our pet projects. The Greeks did not have ideologies. There might have been differences, but in matters of public policy it was a matter of finding solutions. The process, as it was spelled out by Aristotle, was as follows: "[citizens] ask how a policy can be accomplished by what means, and by what means that means can itself be achieved. They do so until they reach the first link in the chain of causes, which is the last in the order of discovery. *Bouleusis,* as described, is thus the pursuit of an investigation."[167]

All too often, political debates at this time of hyperpolarization often start with the answer, with an ideologically colored conclusion, be it less immigration, lower taxation, or higher spending. This is not the best way to engage our brains. There is no investigation and no engagement with other views. We are what we know, and we are not willing to learn.

If we are to truly fulfill our cerebral potential, we need to practice a different kind of politics, one that looks for solutions to established problems. When Aristotle wrote about the Greek city-state, he wrote that we deliberated about things "when we are more uncertain about them."[168]

To solve political problems, we need to focus much more on implementation and less on ideology. This fundamentally means that we must take our fellow human beings seriously. To adopt this attitude, we need to fundamentally revise how we perceive political debates. We have to go beyond the us-versus-them and towards a being-in-this-together approach. That certain institutions can facilitate this is a topic well worth exploring at length. But suffice it to say that the democratic brain needs to focus if it is to live up to its full potential.

Sometimes it has been said that "democracy is a way of life." Tomáš Masaryk (1850–1937), a scholar-politician who became the first president of Czechoslovakia, also defined this system of government as a "discussion." "But real discussion is possible only if people trust each other and if they are trying fairly to find the truth. Democracy is a conversation among equals."[169]

Life is much easier if we simply focus on the ones we like or dislike. But it becomes more difficult if we actually have to rake our brains for practical solutions. That politics is problem solving is something that we often tend to forget. Yet, throughout the ages, those who have written about the art and science of governing a country from a democratic point of view have stressed that this system requires humility and a willingness to learn.

Even your fiercest ideological foe has an evolved brain, just like you. They too are a product of five million-plus years of evolutionary history, in the course of which you both—we all—have become the most sophisticated species that we know. And this has implications for the way we talk to fellow citizens and the way we treat one other. In Liya Yu's words, "recognizing that there exist universally shared brain functions among humans can become a compelling basis from which to establish which cognitive responsibilities different political actors owe each other, irrespective of differences in status and group membership."[170]

Whichever political team you root for, whoever among the politicians you find abhorrent or the opposite, as citizens in a democratic society, we have the opportunity, indeed, the obligation, to contribute to practical solutions. We have a brain that is designed to solve problems through discussion. We do injustice to ourselves if we do not use it.

We grow because we are able to discover by listening. In the brief period when the Netherlands was a democratic republic in the seventeenth century, one of the country's most perceptive minds, the philosopher Baruch Spinoza—a man with a keen interest in early neurobiology, as it happens—wrote that "by consulting, listening to others, and debating, citizens grow more acute, and while they are trying all means, they at last discover those which they want, which all approve, but no one would have thought of in the first instance."[171]

Note that he too saw political decision-making as a journey of discovery and as part of a collective investigation. His argument for democracy was practical and was based on the superior outcomes of allowing people to find solutions. This is still a valid argument. Spinoza, no doubt, would be delighted to hear that there are other arguments for using our brains. We are hardwired to think democratically. We evolved our brains to create societies, arts, and poetry because we have the ability to speak, listen, and learn.

But there is an aspect of this process that we have not looked at so far—another reason why we must encourage *bouleúō*, that is, deliberative listening. For we not only solve problems when we engage in this process of taking counsel. Nor is this process solely to be cherished because it re-establishes the equal worth of others with the same brain as us, though that is important too. The process of engaging our democratic brain is also desirable because it makes us cleverer and even healthier. The more we exercise the brain, the more neurological pathways we keep open, the healthier we get. When we engage our brain in the process of democratic learning, we stay healthy.

So where does this chapter leave us? The answer is simple: if we are to fulfill our brain potential, we need to change the way we do politics; we must move away from hate speech and towards the ideal of *bouleusis*. The art of government is facilitated through a journey of discovery, an investigative process in which we actively engage the speech and especially the listening centers in the brain. That we have this ability is the reason we have been so successful as a species. We need to use this ability—or we may lose it.

Epilogue

Inconclusive Scientific Postscript

"There is room for words on subjects other than last words," wrote my one-time teacher, the late and great philosopher Robert Nozick.[172] This book, in the same spirit, is anything but final. Rather, it is intended to be (almost) the first rather than the last word on neuropolitics.

In the chapters above, the book has introduced a perspective that is still unknown and esoteric to many social scientists. In addition to providing a crash course in social neuroscience and, indeed, in the biology of the brain itself, the book has brought together different strands of this new subfield in political science and neuroscience in a way that not only covers the different areas of research, but also places the endeavors of scholars in historical and philosophical context.

What we have found in this little book is that certain areas of the brain are activated when individuals are engaged in politics (see Box 1) and that there are differences between the brains of conservatives and liberals.

Box 1: Brain Regions Activated in Political Thinking among Conservatives and Liberals

Mostly Conservatives
Amygdala (anger and fear)
Ventral striatum (reward processing)
Dorsolateral Prefrontal Cortex (decision-making and inhibition)
Orbitofrontal Cortex (emotions and social behaviors)

Mostly Liberals
Insula (empathy and disgust)
Anterior cingulate cortex (impulse control and empathy)
Medial Prefrontal Cortex (social cognition)

As the reader will have seen by now, there has been an explosion of research into neuropolitics after new developments in the study of neuroscience were pioneered in the 1990s. Whereas previously, studies of the brain and political attitudes relied on studies of individuals with injuries,[173] technological advances such as fMRI scans (which allow real-time imaging of the blood flow in the brain associated with thinking) have enabled neuroscientists to study what happens inside our heads when individuals are engaged in various activities.[174] Around the turn of the millennium, these studies began to take off in the fields of politics, law, and economics.[175]

More than merely mapping our responses to political statements and the concomitant activities in our brain, this research has also indicated that certain individuals' political attitudes are associated with neural activity in the more primitive parts of the brain (the ones we share with less evolutionarily advanced species). For example, racist attitudes have been correlated with the limbic system, which we share with rats and cats. Conversely, activities in the temporoparietal junction (such as the insula), a part of the brain associated with empathy, sympathy, and the ability to perceive other people's mental states, have been associated with holding more liberal beliefs.[176] (Though we also need to acknowledge that the insula is also associated with feelings of disgust.)[177] But we are still at the earliest of stages, just like mechanics was but an emerging science when David Hume sought to use it as the basis of moral philosophy.

Søren Kierkegaard famously wrote a book entitled *Concluding Unscientific Postscript.*[178] This existentialist writer was pretty far removed from anything associated with a materialist conception of the world, such as the one that underlies *neuropolitics.* And for that reason, perhaps it is appropriate to do the opposite of this self-professed anti-scientific writer. Hence, this final chapter is an *inconclusive* but *scientific* "postscript."

Hopefully, the short introduction to neuropolitics in this book can constitute the first step in a paradigmatic shift towards a (neuro) scientific study of politics. Paradigm shifts, as Thomas Kuhn famously wrote, occur when new theories can explain what old ones could not explain, as well as what they could not account for.[179] Maybe I am too optimistic, but a strong case can be made for the view that neuropolitics fits this description. This is a view shared by others too. Liya Yu, for example, opines that neuropolitical data might already "be able to buttress or even confirm more speculative assumptions held by political scientists about motivating reasons underlying human social perceptions and decision making."[180]

The existing theories of rebellion and revolution are a case in point. While the existing theories can explain part of why some people take part in revolutions, they cannot account for the so-called collective action problem of taking part in a revolution when you can enjoy a free ride.[181]

Rational choice theories—to use but one example—have credible micro-foundations but fail to explain macro-action. The same is true for earlier theories, such as those of Ted Gurr. Neuropolitics, by contrast, provides a rounded and nuanced model of human behavior which is able to incorporate other models and explain why some people rebel, namely, when they are susceptible to being driven by amygdala responses, while others—for falsifiable neurobiological reasons—rely more on the prefrontal cortex.[182]

Further, the theory based on neuroscience can also explain the underlying ideological positions that lead to electoral choices. This again is based on the finding that some people have resources, and that this allows them to have the excess reserves that allow them to act rationally and critically, and thus use the prefrontal cortex. This model goes a long way in explaining the origin of ideological positions, and, indeed, it does so with greater accuracy than the intergenerational models of voter choice that have hitherto dominated the field of electoral sociology.

Further, whereas rational choice scholars have had a difficult time explaining why voters go to the polls, the model based on neuroscience is able to account for this based on dopaminergic explanations, as well as models based on neuroanatomical models that associate voting with pleasure. To be sure, we still need conclusive proof that people get a kick out of voting.

In the earlier days of scientific psychology, the best we could hope for was finding Pavlovian responses prompting action.[183] We can now go a step further and look into the black box of the behaviorists. And through that, we can see—through fMRI scans—that the *nucleus accumbens* is associated not just with reflexes but with desire and motivation as well. There are indications—I wouldn't say proof yet—that this part of the brain is activated when people who are immensely interested in politics are prompted.

Those interested in politics are like salivating dogs; their brains get activated by political stimuli. This finding may not chime with what politically engaged people think, but it provides food for thought that it is strikingly similar to the conclusion reached in the classic sociological study *The Civic Culture* by Almond and Verba in the 1960s. The positive, as opposed to the normative, findings of neuropolitics thus provide a complementary, not an alternative, perspective on political science findings. This does not undermine earlier findings. Rather, it can be seen as a different proof reached through triangulation.

But some findings may be more controversial. In political science, we like to be fair-minded. We—and I think I speak for most colleagues—are acutely aware that we can easily be accused of bias. This sometimes means that we go to absurd lengths to present even outrageous characters in neutral language. This is understandable. We are commentators, not actors in the game. But there is a risk that a *wertfrei*, or non-judgmental, science can become bland. And sometimes it is important not to shy away from statements for fear that they are, or may be, controversial. Political science needs to be objective and not politicized. But what if the insights reveal differences between the two sides of politics that paint one in a better light? Should we avoid saying so for fear of being political?

Whatever you think the answer to these questions is, the fact (sic!) remains that one side of the political spectrum is more driven by emotion than the other. The insights of neuroscience were summed up in an article in *Scientific American*, in which it was stated: "On the whole, the research shows, conservatives desire security, predictability and authority more than liberals do, and liberals are more comfortable with novelty, nuance, and complexity." That is, perhaps, uncontroversial. But the next sentence is not: "the volume of gray matter, or neural cell bodies making up the anterior cingulate cortex, an area that helps detect errors and resolve conflicts, tends to be larger in liberals. And the amygdala, which is important for regulating emotions and evaluating threats, is larger in conservatives."[184]

This is in line with the research we have cited in the chapters above. Liberals, on the whole, use the more sophisticated parts of the brain, whereas some on the radical right resort to amygdala responses. This would seem to suggest that the former are more likely to engage in rational debate than the latter. That might be too strong a conclusion. For we should not forget that the research also shows that conservative voters (and those who, according to Implicit Association Tests, are on the right) tend to have more activated dorsolateral prefrontal cortices—an area that is associated with caution but also with economic thinking. So, it is not all bad for those on the right.

Vous n'avez pas le monopole du cœur—"You do not have a monopoly on the heart"—was French center-right president

Valéry Giscard d'Estaing's riposte to his socialist opponent (and later president) François Mitterrand's when lecturing on the left's commitment to social justice.[185] Elegant, no doubt, and a remark that perhaps helped swing the 1974 election for the conservatives.[186] But from a neuropolitics perspective, Giscard d'Estaing was not on solid ground. Pretty much all the research suggests that liberals—those on the left—are more likely to feel empathy (as an activated insula shows) than are conservatives.

Liberals may not have a monopoly on the insula, but it is not far from being the case. Neuropolitically speaking, liberals are kinder and more likely to use nuanced arguments, whereas conservatives are more prone to rely on evolutionarily more primitive parts of the brain.

Conservatives may be skeptical and cautious, which is a characteristic that has served us well through evolution. Conversely, having empathy has meant that we care for the weak in a way that is unique to the animal kingdom. We need both aspects of the brain to progress further. We are all the product of millions of years of evolution. We all have amygdala responses, and we all have the capacity to use the insula, the dorsolateral prefrontal cortex, and above all, we all have the capacity to listen and talk—in other words, to deliberate over policy issues.

What neuropolitics shows is not just that there are subtle differences in the parts of the brain that get activated when we are prompted, but also that we—alone among species—are social problem solvers. We are an adaptive species, one that learns from interaction with fellow human beings. And this brings us back to the apparent fact that we are hardwired to listen to and learn from each other.

Democracy is discussion and for that you need the ability to discuss and deliberate. What distinguishes us from other animals is our ability to do exactly this, and this gave us an edge in evolution. As a neuropsychologist has put it, "the ability to teach and learn through ways other than through example and imitation [has been a] crucial marker of our success."[187]

Given this, we should perhaps rely more on these skills and less on anger. Maybe we should change our ways and listen to the bard's wise words from *Macbeth* and

"Raze out the written troubles of the brain."[188]

Notes

1   Karl Ove Knausgård, "The Terrible Beauty of Brain Surgery," *The New York Times Magazine*, December 30, 2015, https://www.nytimes.com/2016/01/03/magazine/karl-ove-knausgaard-on-the-terrible-beauty-of-brain-surgery.html.

2   Rudyard Kipling, "The Ballad of East and West," in *Rudyard Kipling's Verse: The Definitive Edition* (Garden City, NY: Doubleday, 1940), 233–36.

3   Liya Yu, *Vulnerable Minds: The Neuropolitics of Divided Societies* (New York: Columbia University Press, 2022).

4   Arnold Howard Modell, "Psychoanalysis, Neuroscience, and the Unconscious Self," *The Psychoanalytic Review* 99, no. 4 (2012): 475–83.

5   Kurt Salzinger, "Inside the Black Box, with Apologies to Pandora: A Review of Ulric Neisser's Cognitive Psychology," *Journal of the Experimental Analysis of Behavior* 19, no. 2 (1973): 369–78.

6   On behaviourism and political science, see James Sloam, "Teaching Democracy: The Role of Political Science Education," *The British Journal of Politics and International Relations* 10, no. 3 (2008): 509–24.

7   Without bragging, I predicted the outcome of the "Brexit" referendum four months before the vote in a peer-reviewed article using these "econometric," or "politometric," models. See Matt Qvortrup, "Referendums on Membership and European Integration 1972–2015," *The Political Quarterly* 87, no. 1 (2016): 61–70.

8   Milton Friedman, "The Methodology of Positive Economics," in *Essays in Positive Economics* (Chicago: University of Chicago Press, 1966), 5, 12.

9   Evidently, I must have done something right, for I was awarded the Prize of the Best Article at the Political Studies Association in 2012 for my article "Terrorism and Political Science" in *The British Journal of Politics and International Relations* 14, no. 4 (2012): 503–17.

10 Matthijs Bogaards, "Coding, Concessions, Conclusions: A Reply to Matt Qvortrup," *Studies in Conflict & Terrorism* 43, no. 10 (2020): 910–12, at 910 and 912.

11 Milton Friedman, *Essays in Positive Economics* (Chicago: University of Chicago Press, 1953), 14.

12 Plato, *The Republic* IV, 439e.

13 Darren Schreiber, "Neuropolitics: Twenty Years Later," *Politics and the Life Sciences* 36, no.2 (2017): 114–31.

14 David Hume, *A Treatise of Human Nature* (Oxford: Clarendon Press, 1896), 1.

15 Marco Magrini, *The Brain: A User's Manual* (London: Octopus Books, 2021), 138.

16 Ingrid J. Haas, Clarisse Warren, and Samantha J. Lauf, "Political Neuroscience: Understanding How the Brain Makes Political Decisions," Oxford Research Encyclopedia of Politics, May 29, 2020, https://oxfordre.com/politics/display/10.1093/acrefore/9780190228637.001.0001/acrefore-9780190228637-e-948.

17 Yu, *Vulnerable Minds*, 74.

18 Hume, *A Treatise of Human Nature* (Oxford: Clarendon Press), 1

19 Plato, *The Republic*, translated with and analysis and notes by John L. Davies and David J. Vaughan (London: Macmillan, 1866), 337.

20 Plato, *The Republic*, 299.

21 Hippocrates of Cos, *The Sacred Disease* (Cambridge, MA: Loeb, 1926), 174.

22 On this fascinating topic, see Bart D. Ehrman, *Heaven and Hell: A History of the Afterlife* (New York: Simon and Schuster, 2021).

23 See René Descartes, *Meditationes de Prima Philosophia*, II.8

24 Benedict de Spinoza, *Ethics*, Part III, Proposition 2. Translated from the Latin by R.H.M. Elwes (1883).

25 See Nicolas Sténon, *Discours sur l'anatomie du cerveau* [1669] (Paris: Classiques Garnier, 2009).

26 John Locke, *An Essay Concerning Human Understanding*, Book IV, Chapter III (London, 1689), 6.

27 Herman Melville, *Moby-Dick; or, The Whale* (New York: Harper and Brothers, 1851), Chapter 10, 55.

28 "The Victorian phrenology craze," *History Extra,* April 21, 2019, https://www.historyextra.com/period/victorian/victorian-phrenology-explain-what-queen-victoria/.

29 As reported in David G. Andrewes, *Neuropsychology: From Theory to Practice* (Abingdon: Routledge, 2016), 516.

30 Dominik Kiser, Ben Steemers, Igor Branchi, and Judith R. Homberg, "The Reciprocal Interaction between Serotonin and Social Behaviour," *Neuroscience & Biobehavioral Reviews* 36, no. 2 (2012): 786–98, at 786.

31 Kent C. Berridge, "The Debate over Dopamine's Role in Reward: The Case for Incentive Salience," *Psychopharmacology* 191 (2007): 391–431.

32 Bryce Weir, "A History of Neurosurgery in Canada," *The Canadian Journal of Neurological Sciences* 38, no. 2: 203–19. Born in Manchester in 1918, Dr. Milner is still active at the age of 104 at the time of writing and is a full professor at McGill University in Montreal.

33 Parinaz Babaeeghazvini, Laura M. Rueda-Delgado, Jolien Gooijers, Stephan P. Swinnen, and Andreas Daffertshofer, "Brain Structural and Functional Connectivity: A Review of Combined Works of Diffusion Magnetic Resonance Imaging and Electro-Encephalography," *Frontiers in Human Neuroscience* 15, article 721206 (2021): 2. DOI: 10.3389/fnhum.2021.721206. See also Christopher J. Honey, Jean-Phillipe Thivierge, and Olaf Sporns, "Can Structure Predict Function in the Human Brain?" *NeuroImage* 52, no. 3 (2010): 766–76.

34 Alexander Romanovich Luria, *The Working Brain: An Introduction to Neuro-psychology* (London: Harmondsworth, 1973).

35 Andrewes, *Neuropsychology*, 19.

36 Luria, *The Working Brain*, 89.

37 For a discussion of the more recent theories of philosophy pertaining to the brain, see Jakob Hohwy, "The Self-Evidencing Brain," *Noûs* 50, no. 2 (2016): 259–85.

38 John Locke, *An Essay Concerning Human Understanding* I.1.8, N: 47 (London, 1689).

39 Pete Seeger, *Dangerous Songs* (Columbia Records, 1966).

40 The *Love Actually* and *Mamma Mia* star commissioned the research when he guest edited BBC Radio 4's *Today* program in December 2022. During the program, he asked scientists to scan the brains of politicians to see if there were any differences depending on their political leanings. As a result of this, the researchers put him on the list of authors. So, it is perhaps slightly overegging the pudding to call him a co-author, though he is listed as such by the other authors of the paper. See "Colin Firth Credited in Brain Research," *BBC News*, June 5, 2011, https://www.bbc.com/news/entertainment-arts-13661538.

41 Shinji Nishimoto, An T. Vu, Thomas Naselaris, Yuval Benjamini, Bin Yu, and Jack L. Gallant, "Reconstructing Visual Experiences from Brain Activity Evoked by Natural Movies," *Current Biology* 21, no. 19 (2011): 1641–46.

42 Rob Waugh, "Brain Scanner 'Reads' People's Dreams – Accurately Enough to See What They Are Dreaming About," *Daily Mail*, October 28, 2011, https://www.dailymail.co.uk/sciencetech/article-2054594/Minds-eye-Experts-use-magnetic-scanner-videos-playing-inside-peoples-brains.html.

43 Georgio Ganis and Julian Paul Keenan, "The Cognitive Neuroscience of Deception," *Social Neuroscience* 4, no. 6 (2009): 465–72.

44 A pioneering study in this regard is Daniel D. Langleben, "Detection and Deception with fMRI: Are We There Yet?" *Legal and Criminological Psychology* 13, no. 1 (2008): 1–9.

45 Ganis and Keenan, "The Cognitive Neuroscience of Deception."

46 Barbara Sahakian interviewed by the author, May 2, 2023.

47 Cara M. Altimus, "Neuroscience Has the Power to Change the Criminal Justice System," *eNeuro* 4, no. 1 (2017).

48 See Michael S. Pardo and Dennis Patterson, *Minds, Brains, and Law: The Conceptual Foundations of Law and Neuroscience* (Oxford: Oxford University Press, 2013).

49 American Psychological Association, "Report of the Task Force on the Role of Psychology in the Criminal Justice System," *American Psychologist* 33 (1974): 1099–1113, at 1110.

50 Based on Robert P. Archer, Jacqueline K. Buffington-Vollum, Rebecca Vauter Stredny, and Richard W. Handel, "A Survey of Psychological Test Use Patterns

among Forensic Psychologists," *Journal of Personality Assessment* 87, no. 1 (2006): 84–94.

51 Nitasha Natu, "This Brain Test Maps the Truth," *The Times of India*, July 21, 2008, https://timesofindia.indiatimes.com/city/mumbai/this-brain-test-maps-the-truth/articleshow/3257032.cms.

52 *United States* v. *Semrau*, No. 0710074 (W.D. Tenn., May 31, 2010).

53 Federica Coppola, "Mapping the Brain to Predict Antisocial Behaviour: New Frontiers in Neurocriminology,'New' Challenges for Criminal Justice," *UCL Journal of Law and Jurisprudence* 1, no. 1 (2018):103 26, at 105.

54 Andrea L. Glenn and Adrian Raine, "Neurocriminology: Implications for the Punishment, Prediction and Prevention of Criminal Behaviour," *Nature Reviews Neuroscience* 15 (2014): 54–63, at 54.

55 Barbara Sahakian and Julia Gottwald, *Sex, Lies, and Brain Scans: How fMRI Reveals What Really Goes on in Our Minds* (Oxford: Oxford University Press, 2017), 53.

56 Matthew Apps, Matthew F. S. Rushworth, and Steve W. Chang, "Anterior Cingulate Gyrus and Social Cognition: Tracking the Motivation of Others," *Neuron* 90, no. 4 (2016): 692–707.

57 J. G. Hakun, D. Seelig, K. Ruparel, J. W. Loughead, E. Busch, R. C. Gur, and D. D. Langleben, "fMRI Investigation of the Cognitive Structure of Concealed Information Test," *Neurocase* 14, no. 1 (2008): 59–67.

58 Jonathan Freedland, "The Road to Somewhere by David Goodhart – a Liberal's Rightwing Turn on Immigration," *The Guardian*, March 22, 2017, https://www.theguardian.com/books/2017/mar/22/the-road-to-somewhere-david-goodhart-populist-revolt-future-politics.

59 For some of these theories, see Thomas F. Pettigrew, "Social Psychological Perspectives on Trump Supporters," *Journal of Social and Political Psychology* 5, no. 1 (2017), 107–16. https://doi.org/10.5964/jspp.v5i1.750.

60 Elizabeth A. Phelps, Kevin J. O'Connor, William A. Cunningham, E. Sumie Funayama, Chris Gatenby, John C. Gore, and Mahzarin Banaji, "Performance on Indirect Measures of Race Evaluation Predicts Amygdala Activation," *Journal of Cognitive Neuroscience* 12, no. 5 (2000): 729–38, 729.

61 Phelps et al., "Performance on Indirect Measures of Race Evaluation, 729.

62 Phelps et al., "Performance on Indirect Measures of Race Evaluation, 729.

63 Phelps et al., "Performance on Indirect Measures of Race Evaluation, 729.

64 See Schreiber, *Neuropolitics: Twenty Years Later*, 123.

65 Drew Westen, Pavel S. Blagov, Keith Harenski, Clint Kilts, and Stephen B. Hamann, "Neural Bases of Motivated Reasoning: An fMRI Study of Emotional Constraints on Partisan Political Judgment in the 2004 US Presidential Election," *Journal of Cognitive Neuroscience* 18, no. 11 (2006): 1947–58.

66 John R. Hibbing, "Ten Misconceptions Concerning Neurobiology and Politics," *Perspectives on Politics* 11, no. 2 (2013): 475–489, at 476.

67 Jaime E. Settle, Christopher T. Dawes, Nicholas A. Christakis, and James H. Fowler, "Friendships Moderate an Association between Dopamine Gene Variant and Political Ideology," *Journal of Politics* 72, no. 4 (2010): 1189-1198, at 1189.

68 See especially John T. Jost and David M. Amodio, "Political Ideology as Motivated Social Cognition: Behavioral and Neuroscientific Evidence," in "Neuroscience of Motivation and Emotion," ed. Eddie Harmon-Jones and Jack van Honk, special issue, *Motivation and Emotion* 36, no. 1 (2012): 55–64, at 60.

69 Bloom quoted in Jost and Amodio, "Political Ideology as Motivated Social Cognition," 56.

70 Jost and Amadio, "Political ideology as Motivated Social Cognition," 57.

71 Xiaojing Xu, Xiangyu Zuo, Xiaoying Wang, and Shihui Han, "Do You Feel My Pain? Racial Group Membership Modulates Empathic Neural Responses," *Journal of Neuroscience* 29, no. 26 (2009): 8525–29.

72 The research design was standard for similar studies. For the benefit of the uninitiated reader, it might be useful to cite the methodology as described by the researchers. It was carried out among seventeen healthy Chinese (8 males, mean 23 years, SD 2.0 years, all right-handed) and 16 healthy Caucasian college students (8 males, mean 23 years, SD 3.7 years, 10 Americans, 2 Dutch, 1 Italian, 1 German, 1 Russian, 1 Israeli, 12 right-handed, 4 left-handed) who were paid for participation. All had normal or corrected-to-normal vision and reported no abnormal neurological history. Informed consent was obtained from all participants before scanning. This study was approved by a local ethics committee. The stimuli and procedure consisted of 48 video clips showing the faces of six Chinese (3 males) and six Caucasian models (3 males). Each clip, subtending a visual angle of 21°/17° (width/height) at a viewing distance of 80 cm, lasted 3 seconds and depicted a face with neutral expressions receiving painful (needle penetration) or non-painful (Q-tip touch) stimulation (Fig. 1a, b) applied to the left or right cheek. After each video clip, participants were instructed to judge whether or not the model was feeling pain by pressing a button using the right index or middle finger. Six functional scans of 204 seconds were obtained from each subject. Each scan consisted of 16 video clips (8 Chinese and 8 Caucasian faces, half with painful and half with non-painful stimulations in a random order). The interstimulus interval between two successive clips lasted 9 seconds, during which participants fixated at a central cross. The last clip in each scan was followed by a fixation of 12 seconds. After the scanning procedure, participants were shown half of the video clips again and had to rate the pain intensity felt by the model ("How much pain do you think the model feels?") and the unpleasantness felt by the onlooker ("How unpleasant do you feel when observing the video clip?") using a Likert-type scale where 0 indicated no effect and 10 indicated maximal

effect (e.g., extremely painful, extremely unpleasant). Xu et al., "Do You Feel My Pain," 8525-26.

73 Xu et al., "Do You Feel My Pain," 8528.

74 Xiangyu Zuo and Shihui Han, "Cultural Experiences Reduce Racial Bias in Neural Responses to Others' Suffering," *Culture and Brain* 1, no. 1 (2013): 34–46, at 34.

75 Zuo and Han, "Cultural Experiences Reduce Racial Bias," 34.

76 Zuo and Han, "Cultural Experiences Reduce Racial Bias," 42.

77 Yuan Cao, Luis Sebastian Contreras-Huerta, Jessica McFadyen, and Ross Cunnington, "Racial Bias in Neural Response to Others' Pain Is Reduced with Other-Race Contact," *Cortex* 70 (2015): 68–78.

78 Cao et al., "Racial Bias in Neural Response," 68.

79 René Descartes, *Discours de la méthode* [1637] (Paris: Vrin, 1987), 10.

80 See Emile G. Bruneau, Nir Jacoby, Nour S. Kteily, and Rebecca Saxe, "Denying Humanity: The Distinct Neural Correlates of Blatant Dehumanization," *Journal of Experimental Psychology: General* 147, no. 7 (2018): 1078–1093. Though it should be noted that Lasana Harris and colleagues conducted "a facial electromyography (fEMG) among a small set of participants, finding that revenge triggered significantly stronger negative emotions against outgroups than dehumanization." See Jordan Kiper, Christine Lillie, Richard A. Wilson, Brock Knapp, Yeongjin Gwon, and Lasana T. Harris, "Dangerous Speech: A Cross-Cultural Study of Dehumanization and Revenge," *Journal of Cognition and Culture* 23, nos. 1-2 (2023), 170–200, at 170.

81 Ricardo Brito and Bernardo Caram, "Bolsonaro Eyes Dividend Tax, Debt Pardon as Brazil Campaign Turns to Economy," *Reuters*, October 7, 2022, https://www.reuters.com/world/americas/bolsonaro-eyes-dividend-tax-debt-pardon-brazil-campaign-turns-economy-2022-10-06/.

82 Anthony Faiola and Gabriela Sá Pessoa, "Bolsonaro hasn't Conceded to Lula. Is he Following the Trump Playbook?" *The Washington Post*, October 31, 2022, https://www.washingtonpost.com/world/2022/10/31/bolsonaro-lula-brazil-election.

83 Ted Robert Gurr, *Why Men Rebel?* (Princeton, NJ: Princeton University Press, 1970).

84 Gurr, *Why Men Rebel*, 257.

85 On unified science, see Otto Neurath, "Unified Science as Encyclopedic Integration," in *Logical Empiricism at Its Peak: Schlick, Carnap, and Neurath*, ed. Moritz Schlick, Rudolf Carnap, Otto Neurath, and Sahotra Sarkar (Abingdon: Routledge, 2021), 309-35. See also John O'Neill, "Unified Science as Political Philosophy: Positivism, Pluralism and Liberalism," *Studies in History and Philosophy of Science Part A* 34, no. 3 (2003): 575-96.

86 Following the defeat of then-president Jair Bolsonaro in the 2022 Brazilian general election and the inauguration of his successor, a mob of his supporters

attacked Brazil's federal government buildings in the capital, Brasília. See "A Copycat Insurrection in Brazil, and Its Troubling Aftermath: The New President Will Find It Hard to Restore Calm, *The Economist*, January 12, 2023, https://www.economist.com/the-americas/2023/01/12/a-copycat-insurrection-in-brazil-and-its-troubling-aftermath.

87 Maciej Równiak and Krystyna Bogus-Nowakowska, "The Amygdala of the Common Shrew, Guinea Pig, Rabbit, Fox and Pig: Five Flavours of the Mammalian Amygdala as a Consequence of Clade-Specific Mosaic-Like Evolution," *Journal of Anatomy* 236, no. 5 (2020): 891–905.

88 For example, *Phaedo* 94b

89 Plato, *Republic*, IV. 440e

90 Communication with the author, April 14, 2023.

91 Plato, *Phaedrus*, in *Plato: Complete Works*, ed. John M. Cooper (Indianapolis: Hackett, 1997), 506–556, at 523 (245a).

92 Plato, *Phaedrus*, 523.

93 Personal communication with Darren Schreiber 14th April 2023. See also, Elisabeth Malkin and Kevin Randall, "Mexico's Governing Party Vows to Stop Using Neuromarketing to Study Voters," *New York Times*, November 11, 2015, https://www.nytimes.com/2015/11/12/world/americas/mexicos-governing-party-vows-to-stop-using-neuromarketing-to-study-voters.html.

94 Shuo Wang, Rongun Yu, J. Michael Tyszka, Shanshan Zhen, Christopher Kovach, Sai Sun, Yi Huang, René Hurlemann, Ian B. Ross, Jeffrey M. Chung, Adam N. Mamelak, Ralph Adolphs, and Ueli Rutishauser, "The Human Amygdala Parametrically Encodes the Intensity of Specific Facial Emotions and Their Categorical Ambiguity," *Nature Communications* 8, Art. No. 14821 (2017): 1–13.

95 Vladimir Humberto Herrera Aquino, "Neuropolítica, una nueva forma de ganar elecciones," *Alcaldes de México*, October 29, 2021, https://www.alcaldesdemexico.com/notas-principales/neuropolitica-una-nueva-forma-de-ganar-elecciones/.

96 Drew Westen, *The Political Brain: The Role of Emotion in Deciding the Fate of the Nation* (New York: Public Affairs, 2008), 61–62.

97 Westen, *The Political Brain*, 62.

98 This is famously argued by Karl R. Popper. For a brief overview, see Karl R. Popper, "Science as Falsification," *Conjectures and Refutations* 1, no. 1963 (1963): 33–39.

99 Jost and Amodio, "Political Ideology as Motivated Social Cognition," 55.

100 Arlie Russell Hochschild, *Strangers in Their Own Land: Anger and Mourning on the American Right* (New York: The New Press, 2018).

101 Antoine Bechara, Hanna Damasio, and Antonio R. Damasio, "Emotion, Decision Making and the Orbitofrontal Cortex," *Cerebral Cortex* 10, no. 3 (2000): 295–307.

102 Woo-Young Ahn, Kenneth T. Kishida, Xiaosi Gu, Terry Lohrenz, Ann Harvey, John R. Alford, Keven B. Smith, Gedeon Yaffe, John R. Hibbing, Peter Dayan, and P. Read Montague, "Nonpolitical Images Evoke Neural Predictors of Political Ideology," *Current Biology* 24, no. 22 (2014): 2693–2699.

103 Personal communication with Dr Darren Schreiber, April 14, 2023.

104 Alexander G. Theodoridis and Amy J. Nelson, "Of BOLD Claims and Excessive Fears: A Call for Caution and Patience Regarding Political Neuroscience," *Political Psychology* 33, no. 1 (2012): 27–43, at 27.

105 Giovanna Zamboni, Marta Gozzi, Frank Krueger, Jean-René Duhamel, Angela Sirigu, and Jordan Grafman, "Individualism, Conservatism, and Radicalism as Criteria for Processing Political Beliefs: A Parametric fMRI Study," *Social Neuroscience* 4, no. 5 (2009): 367–383, at 367.

106 Shirley Fecteau, Alvaro Pascual-Leone, David H. Zald, Paola Liguori, Hugo Théoret, Paulo S. Boggio, and Felipe Fregni, "Activation of Prefrontal Cortex by Transcranial Direct Current Stimulation Reduces Appetite for Risk during Ambiguous Decision Making," *Journal of Neuroscience* 27, no. 23 (2007): 6212–18.

107 Klaus Fliessbach, Bernd Weber, Peter Trautner, Thomas Dohmen, Uwe Sunde, Christian Erich Elger, and Armin Falk, "Social Comparison Affects Reward-Related Brain Activity in the Human Ventral Striatum," *Science* 318, no. 5854 (2007): 1305–1308.

108 Ryota Kanai, Tom Feilden, Colin Firth, and Geraint Rees, "Political Orientations Are Correlated with Brain Structure in Young Adults," *Current Biology* 21, no. 8 (2011): 677–80.

109 Patricia L. Lockwood, Matthew A. Apps, Jonathan P. Roiser, and Essi Viding, "Encoding of Vicarious Reward Prediction in Anterior Cingulate Cortex and Relationship with Trait Empathy," *Journal of Neuroscience* 35, no. 40 (2015): 13720–27.

110 Stephen G. Morris, "Empathy and the Liberal-Conservative Political Divide in the US," *Journal of Social and Political Psychology* 8, no. 1 (2020): 8–24.

111 Kanai et al., "Political Orientations are Correlated with Brain Structure," 677–80.

112 Nicholas O. Rule, Jonathan Freeman, Joseph Moran, John Gabrieli, Reginald B. Adams, and Nalini Ambady, "Voting Behavior is Reflected in Amygdala Response across Cultures," *Social Cognitive and Affective Neuroscience* 5, nos. 2-3 (2010): 349–55, at 349.

113 Darren Schreiber, Greg Fonzo, Alan N. Simmons, Christopher T. Dawes, Taru Flagan, James H. Fowler, and Martin P. Paulus, "Red Brain, Blue Brain: Evaluative Processes Differ in Democrats and Republicans," *PLOS One* 8, no. 2/e52970 (2013): 1–6.

114 Andrew Karpinski and James L. Hilton, "Attitudes and the Implicit Association Test," *Journal of Personality and Social Psychology* 81, no. 5 (2001): 774–88.

115 Kristine M. Knutson, Jacqueline N. Wood, Maria Vittoria Spampinato, and Jordan Grafman, "Politics on the Brain: An fMRI Investigation," *Social Neuroscience* 1, no. 1 (2006): 25–40, at 25.

116 Justine Sergent, Shinsuke Ohta, and Brennan MacDonald, "Functional Neuroanatomy of Face and Object Processing: A Positron Emission Tomography Study," *Brain* 115, no. 1 (1992): 15–36.

117 Knutson et al., "Politics on the Brain," 25.

118 Knutson et al., "Politics on the Brain," 25.

119 Michael L. Spezio, Antonio Rangel, Ramon Michael Alvarez, John P. O'Doherty, Kyle Mattes, Alexander Todorov, Hackjin Kim, and Ralph Adolphs, "A Neural Basis for the Effect of Candidate Appearance on Election Outcomes," *Social Cognitive and Affective Neuroscience* 3, no. 4 (2008): 344–52.

120 Michael L. Spezio et al., "A Neural Basis for the Effect of Candidate Appearance," 344.

121 Anastasia E. Rigney, Jessica E. Koski, and Jennifer S. Beer, "The Functional Role of Ventral Anterior Cingulate Cortex in Social Evaluation: Disentangling Valence from Subjectively Rewarding Opportunities," *Social Cognitive and Affective Neuroscience* 13, no. 1 (2018): 14–21.

122 SW1 is colloquially used to refer to the postal code of British political institutions such as the House of Commons, Buckingham Palace, the House of Lords and Downing Street, to name a few.

123 Personal communication with Mr (now Lord) Blunkett in 2003.

124 Marta Gozzi, Giovanna Zamboni, Frank Krueger, and Jordan Grafman, "Interest in Politics Modulates Neural Activity in the Amygdala and Ventral Striatum," *Human Brain Mapping* 31, no. 11 (2010): 1763–1771.

125 Gozzi et al., "Interest in Politics Modulates Neural Activity," 1763.

126 Gozzi et al., "Interest in Politics Modulates Neural Activity," 1763.

127 Nestor Viñas-Guasch and Yan Jing Wu, "The Role of the Putamen in Language: A Meta-Analytic Connectivity Modeling Study," *Brain Structure and Function* 222, no. 9 (2017): 3991–4004.

128 Soon-Beom Hong, Ben J. Harrison, Orwa Dandash, Eun-Jung Choi, Seong-Chan Kim, Ho-Hyun Kim, Do-Hyun Shim, Chang-Dai Kim, Jae-Won Kim, and Soon-Hyung Yi, "A Selective Involvement of Putamen Functional Connectivity in Youth with Internet Gaming Disorder," *Brain Research* 1602 (2015): 85–95.

129 Gabriel A. Almond and Sidney Verba, *The Civic Culture: Political Attitudes and Democracy in Five Nations* (Princeton, NJ: Princeton University Press, 2015).

130 Roger Dooley, "Do Neuromarketing and Politics Mix?" *Forbes Magazine*, November 20, 2015, https://www.forbes.com/sites/rogerdooley/2015/11/20/do-neuromarketing-and-politics-mix/.

131 Plato, *Protagoras*, in *Plato: Complete Works*, ed. John M. Cooper (Indianapolis: Hackett, 1997), 746–90, at 755.

132 Cicero, "Handbook of Electioneering," in *Cicero: Letters to Quintus and Brutus, To Octavian, Invectives, Handbook of Electioneering*, ed. D. R. Shackleton Bailey, Loeb Classical Library 462 (Cambridge, MA: Harvard University Press, 2002), 421.

133 Dominic Cummings, "On the Referendum #22: Some Basic Numbers for the Vote Leave Campaign," *Dominic Cummings Blog*, January 2017, https://dominiccummings.com/2017/01/30/on-the-referendum-22-some-numbers-for-the-vote-leave-campaign/.

134 Robert Peston, *WTF?* (London: Hodder & Stoughton, 2018), 93.

135 Simone Kühn, Enrique Strelow, and Jürgen Gallinat, "Multiple 'Buy Buttons' in the Brain: Forecasting Chocolate Sales at Point-of-Sale Based on Functional Brain Activation Using fMRI," *NeuroImage* 136 (2016): 122–28.

136 Derek Gleason, "10 Recent Neuromarketing Research Studies with Real-World-Examples," *CXL*, October 2, 2021, https://cxl.com/blog/neuromarketing-research/.

137 Kühn, Strelow, and Gallinat, "Multiple 'Buy Buttons' in the Brain."

138 Laura H. Corbit and Bernard W. Balleine, "Learning and Motivational Processes Contributing to Pavlovian-Instrumental Transfer and Their Neural Bases: Dopamine and Beyond," *Current Topics in Behavioral Neurosciences* 27 (2016): 259–89.

139 H. Hannah Nam, John T. Jost, Michael R. Meager, and Jay J. Van Bavel, "Toward a Neuropsychology of Political Orientation: Exploring Ideology in Patients with Frontal and Midbrain Lesions," *Philosophical Transactions of the Royal Society B* 376, no. 1822 (2021): 20200137.

140 Marios G. Philiastides, Ryszard Auksztulewicz, Hauke R. Heekeren, and Felix Blankenburg, "Causal Role of Dorsolateral Prefrontal Cortex in Human Perceptual Decision Making," *Current Biology* 21, no. 11 (2011): 980–83.

141 On economic decision making and the dorsolateral prefrontal cortex, see e.g., Toshio Yamagishi, Haruto Takagishi, Alan de Souza Rodrigues Fermin, Ryota Kanai, Yang Li, and Yoshie Matsumoto, "Cortical Thickness of the Dorsolateral Prefrontal Cortex Predicts Strategic Choices in Economic Games," *Proceedings of the National Academy of Sciences* 113, no. 20 (2016): 5582–87.

142 Nam et al., "Toward a Neuropsychology of Political Orientation," 2.

143 Junko Kato, Hiroko Ide, Ikuo Kabashima, Hiroshi Kadota, Kouji Takano, and Kenji Kansaku, "Neural Correlates of Attitude Change Following Positive and Negative Advertisements," *Frontiers in Behavioral Neuroscience* 3 (2009): 1–18, at 1. https://doi.org/10.3389/neuro.08.006.2009.

144 Kato et al., "Neural Correlates of Attitude Change," 9.

145 Kenneth Goldstein and Travis N. Ridout, "Measuring the Effects of Televised Political Advertising in the United States," *Annual Review of Political Science* 7 (2004): 205–26.

146 Mary Catherine Bateson, *Willing to Learn: Passages of Personal Discovery* (Hanover, NH: Steerforth Press, 2004), 8.

147 Carl Schmitt, *Der Begriff des Politischen* [1932] (Berlin: Duncker & Humblot, 2015), 25 (author's translation).

148 Abraham Lincoln, *Gettysburg address*, November 19, 1863.

149 James Madison, "Federalist Paper No. 10," in Alexander Hamilton, James Madison, John Jay *The Federalist Papers*, ed. Clinton Rossiter (New York: Signet Books, 2003), 72.

150 Aristotle, *Nicomachean Ethics*, III, iii, 8–11, from the Greek text in Aristotle *Nicomachean Ethics*, translated by H. Rackham (Cambridge: Harvard University Press, 1934), 137.

151 Thucydides, *History of the Peloponnesian War,* 2.34–2.46

152 Aristotle, *Nicomachean Ethics,* 137.

153 Thucydides, *The History of the Peloponnesian War*, 394. (Bk V.89).

154 Thomas Hobbes, *Leviathan: Or the Matter, Forme and Power of a Commonwealth Eccsiastical and Civil* (Oxford: Basil Blackwell, 1946), 112.

155 Barbara Geddes, Joseph Wright, and Erica Frantz, *How Dictatorships Work: Power, Personalization, and Collapse* (Cambridge: Cambridge University Press, 2018), 1-2.

156 Human Development Index, United Nations Human Development Reports, accessed June 22, 2022, https://hdr.undp.org/data-center/human-development-index#/indicies/HDI.

157 Aristotle, *Politics*, trans. H. Rackham (Cambridge MA: Harvard University Press, 1944], (1281b) 222–23.

158 Aristotle, *Politics*, 223, and Robert V. Kozinets, Andrea Hemetsberger, and Hope Jensen Schau, "The Wisdom of Consumer Crowds: Collective Innovation in the Age of Networked Marketing," *Journal of Macromarketing* 28, no. 4 (2008): 339–54.

159 Benjamin Wilson and Christopher Petkov, "Communication and the Primate Brain: Insights from Neuroimaging Studies in Humans, Chimpanzees and Macaques," *Human Biology* 83, no. 2 (2011): 175-189, at 180.

160 René Descartes, *Discours de la méthode* [1637] (Paris: Éditions Sociales, 1950), 90–111.

161 Michael Tomasello, Sue Savage-Rumbaugh, and Ann Cale Kruger, "Imitative Learning of Actions on Objects by Children, Chimpanzees, and Enculturated Chimpanzees," *Child Development* 64, no. 6 (1993): 1688–1705.

162 Patrick J. Gannon, Ralph L. Holloway, Douglas C. Broadfield, and Allen R. Braun, "Asymmetry of Chimpanzee Planum Temporale: Humanlike Pattern of Wernicke's Brain Language Area Homolog," *Science* 279, no. 5348 (1998): 220–22.

163 Source: G. Zamboni, M. Gozzi, F. Krueger, J-R. Duhamel, A. Sirigu, and J. Grafman, "Individualism, Conservatism, and Radicalism as Criteria for

Processing Political Beliefs: A Parametric fMRI Study," *Social Neuroscience* 4, no. 5 (2009): 367–383, at 376.

164 Source: Ashley Lawrence, Michael Carvajal, and Jacob Ormsby, "Beyond Broca's and Wernicke's: Functional Mapping of Ancillary Language Centers Prior to Brain Tumor Surgery," *Tomography* 9, no. 4 (2023): 1254–1275. https://doi.org/10.3390/tomography9040100.

165 Benjamin Barber, *Strong Democracy: Participatory Politics for a New Age* (Berkeley, CA: University of California Press, 1984), 178.

166 Hannah Arendt, *The Human Condition* (New York: Doubleday, 1959), 28.

167 Aristotle, *Nicomachean Ethics*, III,iii, 11.

168 Aristotle, *Nicomachean Ethics*, III,iii, 12.

169 Tomáš Garrigue Masaryk and Karel Čapek, *Masaryk on Thought and Life: Conversations with Karel Capek*, trans. Marie and Robert Weatherall (London: George Allen & Unwin, 1944), 191.

170 Yu, *Vulnerable Minds*.

171 Benedict de Spinoza, "A Political Treatise," in *Benedict de Spinoza: A Theologico-Political Treatise and a Political Treatise*, trans. R. H. M. Elwes (New York: Dover Publications, 2004), 376.

172 Robert Nozick, *Anarchy, State, and Utopia* (New York: Basic Books, 1974), xii.

173 See, for example, Roger W. Sperry, Eran Zaidel, and Dahlia Zaidel, "Self-Recognition and Social Awareness in the Deconnected Minor Hemisphere," *Neuropsychologia* 17, no. 2 (1979): 153–66.

174 See Peter A. Bandettini, "Functional MRI: A Confluence of Fortunate Circumstances," *NeuroImage* 61, no. 2 (2012): A3-A11.

175 See Annabelle Belcher and Walter Sinnott-Armstrong, "Neurolaw," *Wiley Interdisciplinary Reviews: Cognitive Science* 1, no. 1 (2010): 18–22.

176 Libby Jenke and Scott A. Huettel, "Issues or Identity? Cognitive Foundations of Voter Choice," *Trends in Cognitive Sciences* 20, no. 11 (2016): 794–804.

177 Carmelo M. Vicario, Robert D. Rafal, Davide Martino, and Alessio Avenanti, "Core, Social and Moral Disgust are Bounded: A Review on Behavioral and Neural Bases of Repugnance in Clinical Disorders," *Neuroscience & Biobehavioral Reviews* 80 (2017): 185–200.

178 Søren Kierkegaard, *Afsluttende uvidenskabelig Efterskrift til de philosophiske Smuler. Mimisk-pathetisk-dialektisk Sammenskrift, existentielt Indlæg, af Johannes Climacus* (Copenhagen: CA Reitzel, Universitets-Boghandler, 1846).

179 Thomas S. Kuhn, *The Structure of Scientific Revolutions* (Chicago: University of Chicago Press, 2012).

180 Yu, *Vulnerable Minds*, 74.

181 Gordon Tullock, "The Paradox of Revolution," *Public Choice* 11 (1971): 89–99.

182 Shintaro Funahashi, "Prefrontal Contribution to Decision-Making under Free-Choice Conditions," *Frontiers in Neuroscience* 11, art. 431 (2017).

183 As it happens, that model was nowhere near as path-breaking as psychologists believed. Indeed, no less a writer than René Descartes was on to the same idea when he wrote: "If you whipped a dog five or six times to the sound of a violin, I believe that it would howl and run away when it hears that music again" (Passions, 134). But this theory could also be used positively: "If people have at some time in the past enjoyed dancing while a certain tune was being played, then the desire to dance will return to them as soon as they hear a similar tune again" (Passions, 134).

184 Lydia Denworth, "Conservative and Liberal Brains Might Have Some Real Differences: Scanners Try to Watch the Red-Blue Divide Play Out underneath the Skull," *Scientific American*, October 26, 2020, https://www.scientificamerican.com/article/conservative-and-liberal-brains-might-have-some-real-differences/.

185 Valéry Giscard d'Estaing, *Le Pouvoir et la Vie*, vol. 1 (Paris: Compagnie 12, 1988), 401.

186 Before the debate, 50 percent intended to vote for the right; after the debate, the figure was 50.5 percent. See Éditions Chronique, *Chronique du 19 mai*, 6 Jan 2014.

187 Andrewes, *Neuropsychology*, 7.

188 William Shakespeare, *Macbeth*, Act 5, Scene 3.

Subject Index

Name Index

Printed and bound by CPI Group (UK) Ltd, Croydon, CR0 4YY

10/06/2025

14686709-0001